Diary of a Spirit Medium

by

Karen Miranda

RoseDog✹Books

PITTSBURGH, PENNSYLVANIA 15222

ISBN: 978-1-4349-8017-5
eISBN: 978-1-4349-4257-9
Printed in the United States of America

First Printing

For more information or to order additional books, please contact:
RoseDog Books
701 Smithfield Street
Pittsburgh, Pennsylvania 15222
U.S.A.
1-800-834-1803
www.rosedogbookstore.com

Contents

Acknowledgement

To my husband, Charles Miranda, for all of his love and support

To my teachers, Reverend Marie Gaines and Reverend Rita Berkowitz

Thank you, Marie, for your support and care, and being the wonderful teacher that you are.

Thank you, Reverend Rita Berkowitz, for bringing out the best in me as a medium and for your caring.

A special thank you to Mom and Dad

Thank you, Dad, for believing in me.

Thank you, Father Jay, for your spiritual guidance.

I would especially like to thank Fran McGillicuddy for making the writing of this book possible.

Chapter One

The Journey

My story began many years ago in Naples, Italy. My grandfather left Italy in 1918 and came to America to make a better life for his family. His wife had passed away, thus he gathered his few belongings and boarded a boat, like everyone else in those days, which eventually docked at Ellis Island. He got a job as a long shoreman, where he learned five different languages working on the docks. He learned how to speak Polish fluently. This was a man with only a fourth-grade education. Then, he met my grandmother who had two sons of her own from a previous marriage. They moved to Dedham, Massachusetts, and there, they purchased a house. They had a little garden in the back of the house; they even had chickens. My grandfather was a very hard worker. He did not know how to drive a car and couldn't afford one, anyway. He had to walk to and from work. It was quite a long walk from Reedville to Dedham. He also attended night school because he was only educated through the fourth-grade level. He always stressed to his children how important education was because he did not have a chance to get a full education.

My grandmother stayed at home as most women did in those days. She was a very spiritual woman. Together, they had six other children, one of whom was my father. My father, Anthony, did chores around the house, and my grandmother would make special treats for him that he didn't have to share with his brothers. He was not very tall but managed to keep kids away from their property.

My father graduated from high school and got a job at Westinghouse as an assembly worker. There, he met my mother, and a unique relationship began. My mother was an Irish Catholic from Quincy, Massachusetts. My father was Italian, and back then, the Irish and the Italian did not get along well. In fact, to marry someone from a different culture was considered rebellious. During the wedding ceremony, the Irish sat on one side of the room and didn't speak to the Italians. The Italians sat on the other side of the room and didn't speak either. My two uncles had to dance with each other to break the ice.

After the marriage, my father and mother lived with his parents. When they had saved enough money, they bought a house in Norwood. From this marriage, four children were born: three girls and one boy. I am the youngest of the four. I was always shy, and I kept to myself. My best friends were my sister, Joanne, and my dog, Brownie. At the age of eleven, I reached the height of four feet, eleven inches. Little did I know that that would be the tallest I would grow.

One of the special times in my childhood occurred when I was receiving my First Communion at age seven. Throughout the day, I could feel someone's presence in the room. I kept looking over my shoulder, but I could see no one. Even in the car on the way to the church, I could feel it. I wanted to ask my father if he felt anyone around, but I just kept it to myself.

I entered the church and went to the head of the church for the procession to our seats. I loved being in church. I especially liked the stained glass windows. My sister, Dee Dee, came over to say that Sister Elvira was unusually nice to me. Sister Elvira wasn't nice to anyone. Anyway, the music started, and we walked in pairs down the aisle and sat with our families. This was the year that I learned to pray the Rosary, which I continue to do to this day. As I was praying, a nun leaned over and said that there was something special about me. She said, "There is something different about you." I didn't understand what she meant. My mother still talks about that incident from my First Holy Communion. My mother does not forget anything.

Another incident that occurred in my childhood was when I was present at Uncle Nicky's funeral. I witnessed everyone crying, and I could not understand why. I asked my auntie, Clair, why everyone was so sad when Uncle Nicky already told me that he was very happy and living with God in heaven. She asked me how I knew this, and I said, "He told me in my mind when I saw him in the casket." Everyone was very surprised to hear this, and my message made the family feel much better about his death.

My parents had a cottage in Plymouth, Massachusetts. When I was a child, we always went there in the summer. However, the summer before I entered eighth grade was a little different. My grandmother was really sick, and my mother took care of her when she could. We went to Plymouth almost every weekend. We were happy that another school year ended, and we were anxious to go swimming and being free from the tedious nature of school. After swimming and playing with my cousin, I would go to bed. I would fall right asleep, but at about 4:30 A.M., I would occasionally wake up and feel that I was not alone. It was the same feeling I had at my First Communion, when I was seven years old. I would ask who was there, and there would be no answer, but a strange sadness would come upon me. I would feel like I was losing someone close to me. I didn't want to wake up anyone to tell them because they always said it was my overactive imagination. Yet, all I could feel was sadness. I didn't know about clairsentience (the feeling of an unexplained presence) at that time of my life because I was only thirteen years old. I had no idea what these experiences were.

When morning came, I didn't tell my mother about my strange feelings because she would not have believed me. When we sat down for breakfast, the phone rang. The expression on my mother's face changed, and tears filled her eyes. When she got off the phone, my mother told us that our grandmother had passed away at about 5:00 A.M. that morning. I was shocked about hearing the news. When someone you love passes away, it can really upset you deeply. My mother stood there silently. I also hesitated and thought to myself whether someone was trying to tell me about my grandmother's passing the night before. Maybe it was even her saying good-bye to me. It wasn't until years later that I realized I had had a clairsentient experience that morning. We all felt bad about our loss, but we knew my grandmother was not in pain anymore.

When school started up again in the fall, my teacher, Mr. Carroll, told me how sorry he was to hear about my grandmother's death. I thanked him but expressed to him that I was sure she was in a better place. Mr. Carroll became my favorite teacher. He had a genuine caring attitude about all of his students. He made us all feel special and important. After I went to high school, I continued to visit him and his classes.

Life went on normally, or so I thought, until a couple of weeks later, when I felt another presence in the kitchen with me. It was the same feeling as before, as if someone was trying to tell me something. I thought they were trying to tell me that something was wrong or someone was going to die. I couldn't shake this feeling, and I didn't tell anyone what was happening because they would think I was crazy. I just didn't understand what was happening to me. I just kept these experiences to myself.

Back in 1970, we didn't talk about such things as clairsentience, clairaudience, or any psychic experiences, but I could feel when someone I knew was passing. I had the same feeling one day that someone was going to die when I was talking with my father. Then, sure enough, the phone rang, and my father received a message that my mother's sister-in-law had just died. As usual, I was surprised but kept all of this information to myself.

Later on, I found out that someone else I knew had the same gift. My cousin's girlfriend, Nadia, told me to talk about the things that had happened to me when I was growing up because it would help someone else who has gone through similar experiences. This made me think back on all of the experiences throughout my life, and many things came flooding back to me. The events that happened to me as a child started to make sense. I could see a pattern in these experiences, and then, I began to understand what these feelings were. I then realized that everything that happened in the past was connected to the present in some way. I feel that nothing in life is a coincidence.

Everything has a reason and a purpose; we are all connected. Some people can sense these connections, and those are the things that I am writing about.

My spiritual journey continued even though I didn't know I was on one. Looking back, I wonder if the spiritual side of life had plans for me that I didn't know about. I think we decide to do something before we are born into this life, and we receive the help we need to accomplish it.

When my cousin and I were younger, we would often go to family gatherings at Uncle Joe's cottage in Plymouth. We would get bored sometimes, so we enjoyed visiting an old cemetery on a nearby hilltop. My cousin, Joseph, and I loved it there because it was a beautiful place with big, old trees. There was also a big path to walk on that was made up of winding roads that you had to take to get to the top. It felt very peaceful there at the cemetery, and the view was spectacular. I could even see my uncle's house. We would read the old tombstones for hours because they were so old and interesting. We would lose track of time, and I never wanted to leave. I couldn't understand why I loved to go to that cemetery every time we went to my uncle's house. It was like I felt comfortable there, and maybe, I was drawn there to feel the presence of the spirit world.

It wasn't until years later that I would realize my close association with the spirit world. When I started giving readings to people, all of these experiences came together, and I realized that this is what I was meant to do. It is a service I could do for people who were grieving or needing help with their pain. A visit from a loved one can offer immeasurable relief. To know that life goes on is a wonderful message to bring to families and loved ones.

Now, when I do readings, I often see different-colored roses. I see them outside of my head, near the person having the reading. They could be red, yellow, pink, or white. They usually indicate that someone close is having a birthday. Sometimes, the colors indicate certain events that are coming up. Spiritual meanings were getting clearer for me. I saw many more things. I saw spirits of loved ones, and I could hear messages for people. Now, I knew why Joe and I spent hours in the cemetery. I asked him if he knew that I communicate with the spirit world. Joe listened to my experiences since our days in the cemetery, and I am sure he believed that this was meant to be. When I was a child, I didn't realize that all of this would be part of my spiritual journey. The other side had plans for me all along, and I finally understand what all the preparation was for.

As I got older, I was trying to fit in, like most people. I decided to get a job. I went to work as a nursing assistant at the Ellis Nursing Center in Norwood, Massachusetts. It was hard for me because the staff did not like me in the beginning because I worked too slowly. I can remember a nurse called Rita telling me that maybe I should think of doing something else. But I was determined to help people in some way. This time, I knew I could do it because at that time in my life, I enjoyed taking care of the elderly. I can remember a time when giving refreshments and snacks to one of the residents, she said that I must have lied on my application because I certainly couldn't be the age

I said I was. I looked much too young to her. I was seventeen years old, but everyone thought I was twelve years old. I always looked much younger than I was. When I heard her telling her family this, I started chuckling to myself because I should not have been listening to their conversation.

After about a year, I left there and went to Norwood Hospital. Some of my father's friends were patients there, due to heart problems. Since they enjoyed seeing a familiar face, and I really enjoyed working with the elderly, I decided to go back to the Ellis Nursing Center. Needless to say, the staff wasn't too happy to see me, but something was different this time. All of a sudden, I performed my duties easily and the nurse, Rita, was very surprised to see how efficient I had become. Rita ended up liking me very much. As a matter of fact, the nurses on both floors that I worked on had a big party for me when I left to enter the convent. I am thankful to have known Rita; she has since crossed over to the white light. She taught me a lesson about caring for human life, which is one of the hardest jobs one can deal with. It can be a job that no one appreciates. Yet, it has a good side, as I learned along the way.

Chapter Two

Saint Timothy's

Moving on, to a night back in 1986, when I was at church. I belonged to a prayer group, a healing team, and I played my guitar. That is where we did hands-on healing. This was when we put our hands on someone's head or a body part that needs healing, and we pray to God. After the prayer meeting ended, six of us would go upstairs and say prayers with people who wanted healing prayers. I can remember going upstairs and sitting down to pray. There were only a couple of lights on. The church was just the way I liked it, quiet and dimly lit. As I began to pray, the others came up the stairs. Being in the moment of prayer, all of a sudden, I felt someone touch me. When I looked back, there was no one there. I was going to tell my friend, Jeff, not to bother me, because we would joke sometimes, but I realized it was not him. I was a little afraid, but the touch was a soft, gentle touch. It really bothered me that nobody was there. So, I decided to leave the church, but I had forgotten that Jeff was giving me a ride home. Jeff said, "Hey, Karen, where are you going? It's time to do healing, you know?" So, I went back, and he asked me if I was okay. "You look like you wanted to leave." I did not say a word to him about what had happened because I did not want him to think I had flipped my lid. This was a long time ago, back when I did not even know what a medium was, or what signs were there that people had passed away and had gone home to the white light.

Chapter Three

The Convent

One thing I have learned is how things from our past connect to the present. When I was a twenty-one-year-old young woman, a special spiritual feeling came over me. Words cannot describe this feeling. I began wondering if I should enter a convent to become a nun. The feeling came over me so strong that I thought I had heard God's calling. One time, my mother's friend, Betty Sloan, who has since passed, said, "Karen, would you like to go to 'The Centacle'—which is a convent in Brighton where the nuns have spiritual retreat for lay people?"

At the time, I said, "Yes, I would like to go." When the night came, I was looking forward to going.

When we got there, Betty said, "Karen, I have someone I would like you to meet." When we went inside the library, an older nun came in the room. She introduced herself to me. Her name was Sister Mooney. When we were talking, Betty said, "Karen, tell Sister Mooney about what you were thinking about doing. She is the right person to talk with you about religious life."

So, we went into her office, and we started talking. I told her how I would love to become a nun, and she said, "I will help guide you." And so, she let me look at some brochures. And before I knew, it was time to go. I made an appointment to see her again. At that time, I did not even tell my parents what I wanted to do, but I knew there was a time to tell them. When we got home, I said good-bye to Betty, until we got together again. I sat my mother and father down. My mother was happy about the idea. My dad was not, but I was an adult. I said I was going to make a decision soon. My dad started getting used to the idea but did not say anything. When I saw Sister Mooney again, one week later, she said, "Did you like everything in the brochures I gave you?" I said yes, and there was a special section I really liked. Because I had worked with the elderly, I felt drawn to have a vocation in the convent where I would be able to help them. So, we called the vocation director to make an appointment with her. Calling the vocation director is like going for a job interview, but somehow different. When we went up to meet with the sister, my parents also came. After we talked, my mother and father talked to Sister Mooney. My father told her he did not want me to go. Sister Mooney told my mother and father that something was drawing me to the convent, and that it shouldn't be ignored. The sister told me I would have to come up to the motherhouse to take a psychological exam.

The motherhouse was in Avila, on the Hudson in upstate New York. The time came for me to take the test. When we got there, Mom and Dad said their good-byes to me; they would see me in a couple of days. Sister Vincent took me inside. There were three of us who were there for the testing. Then, we met with the novices, nuns who had just begun training. After a tasteless dinner, we went to bed because we had a grueling three days of psychological testing ahead of us. Well, the three days went by, and we were almost done with our test, except that I had missed a whole section. Sister Clara came in and helped me finish the section I had missed. Now I know why they call it psychological testing—it was very emotionally draining. We had to wait for the test results. We began talking about ourselves. The two women and I shared our story of why we were there. Sister Clara came back with the two people who had given us the psychological tests. I was the last to be called in. When one of the women came back, she was upset because she was not a successful candidate. Then, the other one came back, and she seemed upset as well. It was my turn, and I was thinking to myself that I was not going to be chosen because the others had not done well. It was better to get this over with. When I sat down with the sister and the two women who tested me, they said that they believed they were very lucky to be getting me. They thought there was something very special about me. And in a split second, I thought back about what the nun had said to me at my First Communion. She also noticed there was a certain spiritual connection around me. We said our good-byes and did not see each other again until September. I was really excited to have been chosen. They told me to have a good summer, and I thanked everyone and went on my way. The summer could not go by too quickly for me.

Nevertheless, the day finally came—but during the night before, something was different. I could not sleep. I felt a presence, but this time, I did not like what I was feeling. It seemed like a very negative force. It was not until years later that I knew how to protect myself from what I would call "negative energy." Now that I look back, I feel it was a warning not to go into the convent. I didn't know what that premonition was.

When I drove up to New York, my mother and I stopped by to see Father Jay, a really good friend of the family and a close friend of mine. This was the last time I saw him. I began my journey as a postulant, the beginning studies for becoming a nun, and everything went fine for a couple of months. I really did not talk to the other two women who entered the convent with me, but I did talk to Sister Isabella, a senior novice. As time went on, I went to my mother once in a while and told her how I felt at home there, and that everything was going well. There was one time when my mother wrote and told me how, at the prayer meeting, people were being baptized with the Holy Spirit, a special ceremony. The people doing this ceremony were part of a prayer group known as the New Jerusalem. They are a group of people that are more experienced in prayer and healing. So, she asked me if I would say some prayers for the people going through this special ceremony. I said that I would, on Thursday night. Thursday night came, and Sister Agatha turned off all the lights in the chapel, except one. She didn't know that I was sitting there by myself, praying. By now, you are probably thinking what does this have to do with mediumship? If you read on, you will find out. I started praying to the Blessed Mother at the same time that the prayer meeting was starting at my mother's church. Just before I was done, I felt one tear roll down the side of my face. So, I said two more prayers and a special blessing before I left.

A couple of weeks passed, and it was time for my family to visit. It was a nice day outside when they came to visit. But my mother and father came and began talking. When my dad was done, my mother began talking. I had told her how I was praying for the people at the prayer meeting, and one teardrop fell from my eye. At that point, she just looked at me with a surprised look and said, "Karen, during the service, the people all started crying."

I said, "You can send prayers in your own way, and even if it is far away, your prayers will be heard." That was just one of the experiences about healing that I wanted to share.

There were a couple of times that I was pulled into the office for doing some things that I should not do. I was fasting too much, and I failed to go to choir practice when I should have. I often did not complete my laundry chores. I also had to clean the men's lavatory. I felt that these menial tasks were not fulfilling my spiritual purpose. However, I loved the prayer life and taking care of the elderly people. So then, I was thinking, maybe God has something more in store for me. What made it sink in was when I was dismissed from the choir. The dismissal was fine with me because I knew my voice was raspy. When I sang, I would thank God for the gift of life.

Before I left, Sister Isabella came to me, and at the time, I thought she said something very strange to me. She said, "Sister, you are going to suffer a lot."

I said, "Why?" She said that when I was praying, she could see how close to God I was, and she hoped that I was not leaving.

She said, "You belong here." Needless to say, after a year and three months, I ended up leaving the Carmelite Order. At the time, I was hurt about Sister Isabella's comment. But I also knew, at the age of twenty-two, that my heart wasn't in the convent, and that life at the convent wasn't all I wanted for the rest of my life. After leaving the convent, I felt that my time there made me more caring and empathetic toward other people's feelings. However, I continued on my spiritual journey.

When I arrived home from the convent, I felt as if I was living in the dark ages. People were not very nice to me. Some of the parishioners from my home parish was very disappointed because I left the convent. They were rude and arrogant about my perceived failings.

I can remember being in church at St. Timothy in Norwood, Massachusetts, and after the Mass was finished, one of the parishioners came over to me, looked down on me, and said, "You came home." And she stuck her nose up in the air at me. She made me feel disgraced and unwelcome. She made me feel even worse than I was already feeling at that time in my life. It was the lowest point in my life.

Then, my mother came over to me and said, "Karen, would you like to go to Israel?" I told her I would love to go. "We will meet with the group from Sacred Heart Church in Quincy, Massachusetts, and we will go to Logan Airport with Father Tom."

When we went to Israel for a couple of weeks, Father Tom told us that we were going to Mount Carmel. The next day, I looked at my mother. She looked at me, and I told her I am not sure about going to Mount Carmel because of how the Carmelite Sisters of the Aged and Infirmed at the convent had made me feel when I was there. The next day came and off we went, and as we got close to Mt. Carmel Church, I didn't want to go in. It was a beautiful, clear day; the weather was nice. When we got in the church parking lot, I told my mother that there was no way I was going in there. I was still upset by my treatment in the convent.

My mother got Father Tom, and he tried to talk me into going inside the church. Nevertheless, I just didn't want to listen to one word he had to say to me. Sometimes, I can be very stubborn. So, I just sat in the bus. Then, a very nice lady named Emily came over to me and started talking to me. She told me, "Karen, why don't you go in and pray for the nuns?" And I got to thinking about what she said to me. I got off the bus. It was something that Emily told me that got me thinking. The church was big and beautiful. Father Tom looked very surprised to see me. Father Tom surprised us by telling us he was going to have a Mass there. We went upstairs, to the main part of the church, and we saw the beautiful stained glass windows and paintings on the walls. Well, Mass started, and we all began to sing; it was the first time I had sung since the convent. We got to say some prayers during the Prayers of the Faithful, and it was very quiet. I can remember looking up, toward the ceiling, and seeing the sun beaming through the windows. It was like the heavens were opening—and peace reined. It was so quiet that you could hear a pin drop in the room. Father Tom said that it is time to pray and asked if anyone have a special request during the Prayer of the Faithful (a time when special prayers can be requested). I said that I would like to pray for all the nuns, especially for the nuns who were not nice to me when I was in the convent.

When Mass was over, two women came over to me, and they said, "Do you have a minute to talk to us?" I said I did. One of the women said to me, "I was in the same order as you were, the Order of Nuns for the Aged and

Infirmed, and the same thing happened to me." The nuns were not nice to her either. And when she left, she was in the final of the three levels to becoming a nun. I looked at her and smiled, and that was very healing for me. The rest of the trip went fine, and the Bible was never the same for me again; it came alive. I never ran into the lady again, but she will never know the impact she had made on me and how healing it was. Life went on for me, and now, I look back and know that it was a life lesson. Because of this experience, I am now more caring toward other people's feelings.

Chapter Four

Jeannie

As life continued on for me and I became used to being at home again, I knew I had to go back to work. I decided to go back to work as a nursing assistant. I went to the Charlwell Nursing home; that was just up the street from where I lived. I put in a job application, and the nursing home director hired me right on the spot.

As I got used to my new job, I also got caught up with some of my old friends. My old friends were very happy to see me, and at the same time, I began making some new friends. I also started dating. I know you are probably saying: Dating? At first, some of my family members were surprised to hear that I was dating. I told my family members that life went on after the convent.

One day, we had a really busy morning at work, and I was very happy to see lunchtime come. When I got down to the lunchroom, I saw this girl over at one of the tables eating, so I went over and introduced myself to her. Little did I know at that time, we would become very close friends. One day during lunchtime, I saw Jeannie, and I asked her if she would like to go out night-clubbing with me and some of my other friends that night. She told me yes. When we went out to Frank's—that was one of the nightclubs in Stoughton, Massachusetts, at that time—we all got up and went onto the dance floor. Then, a couple of other friends of mine came into the club, Buster and his friend, Dannie.

As we were all talking, Dannie asked me, "How come Jeannie always wears her hair the same way all the time?" I looked over at him, and I told him I didn't know. At that time, I had only known Jeannie for about a year, and I wasn't about to ask someone who I really like why she wears her hair the same way all the time.

The next day, Buster called me, and I told him how Dannie had upset me when he asked about how Jeannie liked to wear her hair. I knew that it isn't anything to get upset about, so I continued talking to Buster, and I told him that one day, when I feel comfortable, maybe I would ask Jeannie why she always wore her hair the same way, but for now, I did not want to say anything to her. One night, Jeannie and I went out to eat and to the movies. It was a very windy night, and when we were walking, my hair was blowing all over the place. When I looked at Jeannie, I noticed that when her hair was blowing in the wind, there wasn't any hair there.

Then, I came right out and asked her, "Why do you wear your hair the same way all the time?" hoping that I wouldn't upset her.

She looked over at me very seriously and said to me, "Karen, someday, I will tell you why, and you will know then." I had a feeling that something wasn't right, and I never brought the subject of her hair up with her again. The following day came, and I went to work and then out that Saturday night. When I got to Frank's with my other friends, I called Buster aside, and I told him about the phone conversation I had the night before with Jeannie. All Buster did was listen, and I told him that I would never ask Jeannie again why she wore her hair the same way. Then, I told Buster that it wasn't my business anyway, and that if Dannie wanted to know, he could ask her himself. I liked Jeannie, and I never asked her again.

Since then, I met and became engaged to a man named Chuck. We got invited to go to a wedding out in Denver, Colorado; one of Chuck's friends was getting married. We decided to go on the trip. The flight was only a couple of hours, but when we got there, I was very sleepy. I forgot that Denver was above sea level. The day of the wedding finally came, and it was beautiful. We could feel the fall in the air.

The next day, we went to see some of the rocks and the little villages that were next to the mountains. I can remember going in one of the gift shops and getting a crystal heart. Before we knew it, it was time for us to leave. So Ed, Chuck's friend, drove us to the airport. We once again congratulated him on getting married, and then, we said our good-byes. On the way home, I started falling asleep and was a little uneasy about something. All at once, I closed my eyes and went to sleep. My friend, Jeannie, came into my dream. Then, I knew that there was something very wrong. This happened one other time, when my friend's sister's mother had passed away. I didn't say anything to Chuck.

We finally landed at Logan Airport, and it was good to be back in Boston, Massachusetts again. After I arrived home, I still couldn't shake the feeling that there was something terribly wrong with my good friend, Jeannie, whom I had known for four years. We went to get our luggage, and then, I said to Chuck, "Let's go meet my father at the gate where he was waiting for us."

When I took a look at his face, I knew there was something wrong. We all got into the car, and it was very quiet. The radio wasn't even on even though, usually, one is very excited when you come home from a trip. Nobody said a word, and I do mean not a word was said. Then, my father said, "Karen,

Jeannie is very sick. Something is terribly wrong with her." Needless to say, the rest of the ride home was very quiet. Chuck and I said our good-byes to each other, and he told me he would call me the next day. When I got into the house, my mother told me that Maureen (a friend of Jeannie's) called and was very upset. Maureen has since passed.

I didn't know what was going on with Jeannie, so I decided to call the Regans. They told me the news that Jeannie's cancer had come back, and that she was in the hospital. Then, I knew why she wore her hair the same way all the time: because the radiation treatment makes you lose your hair. She had had a brain tumor ever since she was four years old.

This would be the time that I needed to spend with my friend. I was lost for words, but I asked God to give me the strength to be a good friend to her. Then, I called her at the hospital. My friend suffered a long, hard battle with cancer but never gave up the fight to live, and I do mean live. She would be back and forth to the hospital for treatments until she couldn't go anymore.

As time went on, I ended up breaking up with the man I was engaged to. Then, a year later, in 1988, I met my husband, Charles, and yes, another Chuck.

My friend, Jeannie, did get to come to my wedding, but couldn't take part because of her cancer. Her cancer got worse, but when I came home from my honeymoon, she was still with us.

When I was expecting my son, her condition started getting even worse. Her eye didn't look the same, and I made off like I didn't even know what was going on, so that my friend wouldn't feel different.

She ended up in the hospital again, and they had to close her eye up due to her cancer. She was at New England Medical Center in Boston. One thing about Boston is that they have some of the best hospitals in the world.

So, Chuck and I went to see her. I told her about Paul, the baby, and how he was a blessing to me. When we were finished seeing Jeannie, we were to see my uncle, Larry, who was having surgery at the time. Due to cancer, Uncle Larry also passed away, just a couple of years later.

As life continued, I gave birth to another baby, a girl, who we named Melissa. I took her with Chuck and Paul to see Jeannie. She couldn't get out of bed anymore because her cancer had progressed so badly on her face. It was Halloween, and we brought her some pumpkins, but before we went up to see her, her mother and father told us that her face wouldn't be an easy thing to look at. I wanted to go up anyway because she was my friend. It was very hard seeing her that way. Chuck couldn't stay in the room. He couldn't see her that way, but I stayed. I even let her hold the baby, and she smiled about that. I looked over and saw the pumpkins I had given her at Halloween, and they were still like brand new. All I could think of was that they were there because my friend's birthday was near Thanksgiving.

My heart was breaking inside to see someone so young and very nice dying such a horrible death. And little did I realize that that visit would be for the last time. She shared something with me, which took me off guard—because I didn't think she could remember the past. They were private things that I would always keep private, but hearing her tell me I was right about something that I said to her made me feel more at peace.

Time went quickly, and before we knew it, hospice came to help her. They are a wonderful organization that should be more recognized by people for the wonderful work they do to help people who are dying or terminally ill. We would say our good-byes for the last time. Time went by so quickly, and soon, it was springtime. Chuck and I went up to my parent's house with the babies.

When we were there visiting, it happened: The phone rang, and it was my friend, Flo. She called to tell me that my friend, Jeannie, had passed away suddenly. When we got the news, my mother said to me, "Karen, why don't you and Chuck go visit the Regans?" We said we would, and then, the phone rang again; it was Jeannie's sister, Maureen. She told us the news again, and I told her that we were on our way over, and that we would be there very soon.

When we got there, Mr. Regan was there to greet us and was very happy to see us. We went inside and all sat down. They told me how Jeannie had pneumonia, and that's what got her in the end because she had no immune system left due to her cancer. Mr. Regan told me that Jeannie's mother was with Jeannie when she had passed away. She fell asleep in her mother's arms that night, and that was the saddest thing I had ever heard. I was trying to hold all the feelings back, so I could listen to what they had to say.

Then, when we got ready to leave, I walked out with Mrs. Regan. I could see her sadness at losing Jeannie. All I could say was, "I know what you are thinking. You are supposed to be the one to die first, not your child, no matter what someone's age was." She smiled at me and said I was right. I said my good-byes to Jeannie's parents and told them that I would keep them in my prayers and see them at the wake.

Well, I didn't make it to the wake or the funeral. I was very upset about that, but I had no way to get there, and I had two little babies depending on me.

My landlord, Al, knew I was very sad. He knocked on my door and said, "Karen, when you have a minute, can you come up to see me?" So, I told him okay. I got the babies, and we went upstairs and sat down. He looked at me, smiled, and told me, "You were there when your friend needed you, right?" I told him yes. There were others who were not there for her and others who hardly ever called her. He told me that I didn't need to be at the wake or the funeral, anyway. I thought that was such a strange thing to say to someone. He said, "I know it doesn't make sense, but you did what you could as a friend when she needed someone the most." This made me feel a little better. I told him how all my other friends were there except for me, and he told me they needed to be there. He told me that I didn't need to be there, and that I could say good-bye in my own way. Little did I know that someday, I would be telling people the same thing.

Well, like everything else, life continued on. Summer came and went, then fall, and before you knew it, it was Christmastime. I was decorating the apartment for Christmas, and I came across this red candle. It had a light on it, but I didn't turn it on. I couldn't because it was something special to me. Jeannie had given it to me the previous Christmas. So, I put it on the fireplace when I was cleaning the dishes. Something strange happened. The light went on all by itself. Chuck came in from the store and said, "Hey, Karen, you put the light on too early; it isn't dark yet." I wanted to tell him I didn't put it on, but I kept it to myself. I let it burn out by itself; it stayed on for just a couple of days.

Winter was over, and it came close to Mother's Day. When Mother's Day came, it got really busy. When I was in the kitchen, something kept telling me to call Jeannie's mother and wish her a happy Mother's Day. Then, I felt like I was not alone, and that there was someone else in the room with me. It reminded me of the time when I was down in Uncle Charlie's house and how I could feel him, but there was nobody there.

So, I fluffed it off. Then, it happened again! *"Call my mother and wish her a happy Mother's Day."* It was coming in soft but persistent in my head.

Then, I said, "Jeannie, is that you? I feel you around me." The voice came again. It was the first anniversary since my friend's death. I said, "All right, I'll call her." When Mrs. Regan answered the phone, I said, "Hi, this is Karen." I could tell she was happy to hear from me. Then, I told her, "Please don't think I am being strange, but I am supposed to wish you a happy Mother's Day. Jeannie wanted me to call you."

The phone got silent on the other end, and she told me, "Karen, I was just thinking of her." She was happy to get the message. We talked for a while, and I told her that I knew Jeannie was around us. I know that the first anniversary is one of the hardest. It doesn't get any easier as the years go by. For some people, it is just different.

I never saw my friend's mother and father again. Like many things in life, sometimes, we just drift away from people we know.

I hadn't thought of my friend for a couple of years, until one day, on October 1, 2005, I had just finished watching *It's a Miracle* before falling asleep. Jeannie came into my dream, and all at once, the living room lit up. My sister's hope chest started blinking on and off, and I knew she was around. That is one thing I have learned as a medium; when I was sitting here writing this story on October 30, 2005, my kitchen light started blinking on and off. I said hello to my good friend, knowing that she was healthy on the other side, not in any more pain, and letting me know that she is still around me spiritually.

Chapter Five

The White Light

It was the summer of 1988. I recall that this summer was extremely hot. At the time, I was dating my husband, Charles. It was a blazing-hot day, and I asked my parents if it would be all right to visit their cottage in Plymouth in order to swim in the lake. They said it was fine, so we went. As soon as we arrived, we put on our bathing suits and jumped into the water. Chuck didn't know how to swim, so he stayed in shallow water. After we got out of the water, we saw my mother and aunt. They invited us to the four o'clock Mass. Chuck declined the offer, but I was eager to join them. It was beneficial for Chuck to stay behind and have some quality time with my father.

Once we got to Saint Peter's, I again realized how hot it was. The church was crowded, and the air was thick. Although the weather conditions were unbearable, I enjoyed the old, well-decorated church. The harmonious music began, and Mass started. As the priest started his sermon, something caught my attention. The window above the right side of the altar was harboring a beam of brilliant white light. It was the most beautiful thing I had ever seen. To make sure this was not a problem with the heat or my vision, I rubbed my eyes, but the light remained. I quietly looked around the church to see if anyone else was witnessing this spectacular event, but nobody seemed to notice. I never told anyone about this experience until many years later. It occurred again at my daughter's First Holy Communion. The children were praying, and above them shone a brilliant white light. This time, it was mixed with sparkles of gold. It was so stunning. I could not believe my eyes. As the children sat down after communion, the light engulfed them with sparkles of gold and white light. Once again, I surveyed the church to see if anyone else was experiencing this, but it seemed as though they were not. I told Chuck what was going on, but he could not see it. He said that I looked so peaceful.

He went on to say that he loved seeing me so happy. A nun had told me one time that I was special, and now, I began to believe it. I wonder how she knew that I had a gift for these unusual experiences. I never told anyone except my husband, Chuck, about these experiences, and not until I started to develop as a medium. There was much to be discovered, and I wondered what God had in store for me.

Chapter Six

Dreaming Sister Mooney

Back in 1985, early in the morning, I had a dream. All at once, there was someone with me whom I hadn't heard from in a long time. Her name was Sister Mooney. She helped me when I went into the convent. She was dressed in her habit, had a big smile on her face, and sitting in her rocking chair. Suddenly, she leaned back and went to sleep. I knew at that point that she had left her body, simply by the feeling I had. Later that morning, I went to work. When I returned home, my sister told me that she had something to tell me. Before she could tell me, I told her that I already knew. I told her that Sister Mooney had passed away. Well, you should have seen the look on my sister's face. Later on, I did tell my mother what had happened, and she was happy that the sister had let me know that she would not be with us anymore.

One of the ways that people who have crossed over to the white light reach us is through our dreams.

Chapter Seven
The Honeymoon

I would like to talk about Uncle Charlie. We all used to say he had nine lives. He had been through a lot when he was in WWII. He was there when they blew up Pearl Harbor; he was on one of the boats in the harbor. He also survived an aneurysm in his head and made a full recovery. When my husband and I were married, on June 10, 1989, we went to Aruba for one week. When we came home, we went down to Craigsville on the Cape for a week. As the sun was setting, I started to feel a little uneasy. Chuck wondered what was wrong with me. I said, "Chuck, we are not alone." He wondered what I meant. I felt like Uncle Charlie was with us. Chuck did not know who Uncle Charlie was, except he did know we were at his beach house, and that he had crossed over. This was way before I knew what a medium was. We ended up staying at a hotel because I just could not shake the feeling that my uncle, who had passed away, was watching over us.

The next day, Chuck had to go out to the car to get some of the things we had left there the prior night. When he came back to the room, he told me that he had some bad news. He had locked the keys inside the car. Chuck called the police, and they were able to unlock the car door without damaging it. After all was said and done, we went back to my uncle's house. Chuck asked me if I was okay about going back inside. I told him that I think my uncle had already left because I could not feel his presence any longer. As our conversation continued in the car, I told Chuck about Uncle Charlie's funeral that took place in 1987, on Memorial Day weekend. When we returned to my mother's home in Norwood, Massachusetts, there was no one in the house. However, there was one thing that caught my attention. I remember that when we left the house for the funeral, the electricity was shut off. When we returned, the television was on and filled with snowy static.

We all looked at each other with puzzled expressions, and we could not understand how it had happened. I learned that when my uncle passed to the other side, he was in his recliner watching the late-night show. Chuck just listened, and he said it was very interesting. At that point, my friend, Patrick, pulled up in my uncle's driveway; he and his wife had come to stay at the beach house with us for a couple of days. I was a little afraid to go back into the house. That was the last time that I heard from Uncle Charlie. At least, that was what I thought—until fourteen years later!

This happened another time, before Chuck and I got married. It was in 1988, when I met Chuck. We had been dating for about six months. Chuck and I were visiting his father. We all called him Papa. Chuck grew up in Chelsea, Massachusetts. Once when we were in the living room, I looked at Chuck, and he said, "Karen, what is wrong?" I told him I saw a woman in her late forties near the left-hand side of the window. She had on a long, off-white nightgown. She was smoking a cigarette, and she was not tall in height. He just looked at me and said, "Karen, that was my mother. But you didn't even know her."

I said to him, "I know, but I can feel her, and she is standing right over there." It was not until years later I found out that this experience was both clairsentience and clairvoyance. Clairsentience is when you can feel the presence of people who have crossed over; clairvoyance is when you can see them. Before the honeymoon, my mother-in-law, Rose, had let me know that she was around on more than one occasion. My sister-in-law, Jeannie, had validated this more than one time. She had lots of nice energy. I did not know her when she was alive and sick, but I had come to know she was spiritually healthy. Once in a while, my husband would say, "But Karen, you did not even know my mother at all." Then, I would have to ask Bobby or Jeannie just so someone could understand her. Until this day, once in a while, Chuck gets a little skeptical of me, even though I am usually correct. But that is okay.

Chapter Eight
Being Diagnosed with Multiple Sclerosis

One day, we were watching TV, and my husband, Chuck, came home early. He surprised me when he said, "I have something to tell you."

I asked him, "What?" He said my uncle, Larry, had passed away. I felt sad hearing the news. Earlier that day, I had a bad headache. I just had a new baby girl six months earlier. My headache was so bad that I had to lie down next to the baby. I told my husband about it, and he took me to the hospital right away. The hospital was of no help to me. I made an appointment with my primary doctor a few days later. The day of my doctor's appointment was the same day of my uncle's funeral. We all went to the church, saddened about our loss. It was a beautiful spring day, not even one cloud in the sky. We all gathered and went inside the church. The priest said the opening prayer, and as the service went on, I felt a presence, like I wasn't alone. When the Mass was over, we went to the cemetery, and Chuck said to me, "Karen, would you like to go to the grave?" I couldn't go, so I stayed back with the baby. I told Chuck that my uncle wasn't there anyway. Chuck looked at me, I looked at him, and he said, "What a strange thing to say."

We went back to my cousin's, Bill's, house. My doctor's appointment was scheduled for three o'clock. My aunt, who was married to Larry, came over and sat next to me. I told her that I was going to miss Larry, my phone buddy. This was a special friendship I had with Uncle Larry. When there was something wrong, he would call me and let me know. He would say, "Don't tell anyone." One thing I was always famous for was *not* keeping a secret. So, I would call my father and tell him something was wrong. They would be glad that they knew. I never told them how Dad found out.

Before you knew it, it was time to go to the doctor. I just looked at my aunt and told her that he is no longer in pain, and that he is in a good place.

We went to the doctor's office. The doctor said, "Karen, walk in a straight line." But I couldn't. My husband tried to be funny and said that walking in a straight line was a hard thing to do. Everyone laughed. The doctor said he'd be sending me for an MRI (Magnetic Resonance Imaging). The appointment was made for the following morning. The day of the test came, and I went. Before the test, something said to me to pray to the Sacred Heart of Jesus. I was thinking, *This is nuts*. When I went inside to have the test, I felt something touch me, and the voice came back again. The voice said, "Stick with me." I thought I flipped my lid. I thought if I told anyone about this, I would end up in the cracker factory. After the test, I went to my mother's house before I went home. Something was pushing me to call my aunt, Uncle Larry's wife. So, I called her and asked her if Uncle Larry ever prayed to the Sacred Heart of Jesus. The call was silent, and then, my aunt started to cry. She said that no one knew that Uncle Larry did pray to the Sacred Heart of Jesus. When I was done talking to my aunt, I had to take care of something before I went back to Norwood.

The next day, the phone rang. It was the doctor's office. They said it was good news. There was no bleeding in the brain, but since it was the weekend, the doctor would get back to me on Monday. On Monday, the doctor called and told me that there was fluid in my brain. I had to go and see a neurologist, so another appointment was made for this.

The next day, we went to the neurologist, and he showed me the MRI. He asked, "What illnesses run in your family?" I came back with, "Everything but Parkinson's." Then, he asked what disease is more prevalent than any other in the family tree. I said Multiple sclerosis. Then, he told me that I had MS. The next step would be that I had to get treatment.

I followed up the next day with a five-day treatment plan. With my husband by my side, I started the next morning with the treatments. After the nurse got me hooked up with everything, my husband asked me, "Would you like a cup of coffee?" Then, he left the room. I looked over at the baby, and as I looked up, I said to God, "I don't have time for this." I looked in the doorway of my room and felt a presence and a voice saying to me, "Pray to the Sacred Heart of Jesus." I could feel Uncle Larry near. After the first treatment, we went back to my mom's house, and we all sat down to eat.

My mom started to talk about Uncle Larry. So, I took advantage of the conversation. I said to her, "Did someone say 'stick with me, kid'?"

My mother looked at me and asked, "How did you know that?" My uncle said it to them all the time when they were small. It was one of his favorite sayings. My mother said that she didn't want to talk about it anymore because it freaked her out.

In the fall of 1999, it was time for my checkup with the neurologist. I went in to take my shower, and as I closed my eyes, I heard my aunt, Rita (who has passed on), saying, "Karen, get the relic of St. Theresa out." But I did not have it on me. My mother did. I called my mother, and she asked why I wanted that. I did not want to tell her how Aunt Rita spoke to me. I remembered her reaction after I told her about Uncle Charlie. So, I said to her nicely, "Could you please get it out for me?" Then, I told her that I would see her very soon.

Then, Aunt Rita came back again, and I heard her say, "Karen, get your rosary out and the piece of palm you got on Easter Sunday." So, I did, and I thought, *Here we go again*. On the way up to my mother's house, I started praying with the rosary.

I do not think Chuck knew what to make of me. He said, "Whatever you need to do, Karen, go do it." So, I said, "Can you please turn off the radio." And to my surprise, he said okay.

When we arrived at my mother's house, my mother said, "Karen, here is the relic. What are you going through?" But I did not pay attention to her. I said thank you, and we went on our way. When we got to the hospital, I continued to pray. But I could not take the rosary or the relic in the MRI room due to the radiation.

So, after the MRI, we went back to my mother's house, and my mother just gave me a look. Then, I asked her, "Did Aunt Rita pray to St. Theresa?"

She just looked at me, smiled, and said, "Yes, how did you know?" I did not answer her that day, remembering what had happened the last time. Then, the waiting started. We started waiting for the test results to come in.

Monday came; the phone rang, and I answered the phone, being very nervous about the test results. The secretary was very happy with the news. She told me, "Some of the damage from the MS is healing. We are not used to telling people that they are doing better." So, I got off the phone, looked toward the ceiling, and said, "Thank you, God." The doctor told me to keep doing what I was doing. Today, I have been in remission for five and a half years. It is like getting a second chance at life. That is why, during the day, or when I wake up in the morning, I thank God for allowing me to walk. Prayer, to me, is a big part of healing, but it is nice to know that our family and friends on the other side are watching us and guiding us.

Chapter Nine

The Tearoom

When this entire situation started going on, I was very quiet. One day, all of my friends told me about the tearoom. The tearoom is a place where people go for readings. I said to Carol, "Okay, I will go with you."

The next day, we went, and they had a resource book with a list of all different readings. One of the girls said, "This one looks like a good one." It was called a spirit reading.

I looked at them and said, "That sound's right to me." Little did I know. So, I went for a regular card reading. This is something we did just for fun. After I was done, I went to the waiting room, and when they came out, they were both crying. I said to them, "Are you okay?"

They said, "Yes."

On the way home, they told me I should go, so I said, "I will." The next day, I made an appointment with what they called a spirit reader. She started talking, though she was a little nervous. I waited to hear what she had to say. She started telling me about a dog named Sandy. With a surprised look on my face, I knew who it was. It was my friend's—Jeannie's dog. I waited until she was done and said to her that, "Once, Michelle woke up at 2:00 A.M. for a feeding. I sat in my rocking chair. I felt like there was someone on the stairs looking at me (which is known as a clairsentience, a feeling of someone who has passed being near)." She told me that she was around me and guiding me. Little did I know that, even then, I was bound to be a medium. After that, strange things began to happen to me. I would see a glimpse of people who had crossed over. I didn't understand what was going on. Then, I was diagnosed with MS. So, I just looked at everything as a coincidence, but I knew that nothing really was. Things did continue, so I decided to make an appointment to go back to the tearoom.

One of the other readers there, who is very good, said she knew that I had the gift. She told me what was going on with me. I said, "This is nuts." But, she was right.

She said, "I am not saying to you to keep coming for readings because if you think you have this gift, there are places you can go." This is how I found out about the Spiritualist Church in Quincy. I was led to this church later on. When I went to this church, it was to learn, grow, and control this gift of mediumship that God had given to me to help others.

Chapter Ten

The Spiritualist Church and Spiritualism

After going for a reading at the tearoom, I was led to the Spiritualist Church in Quincy. When I first started going, it was uncomfortable for me. Because I was brought up as a Roman Catholic, I was drawn to one way of understanding what was happening in my life. I continued to go to the church and began taking classes. The teacher would say that nothing but the white light should guide and keep us safe and protected. At that time, there was only a small group of people; each of us had our own gifts in our own way. Before you knew it, all of our energy came together. What I mean by this is that some people in my development class could hear spirits, and this is called clairaudience; other people could feel spirits, and this is called clairsentience. Some people could see spirits of people who passed way, and this is called clairvoyance. Each one of us had a gift of spirit communication. I did not even know what a medium was; I knew that I needed to understand what was happening to me. When I stopped attending my development class on Tuesday night, I kept myself busy with everyday activities, trying to be as normal as possible, including singing in my old church choir on Wednesday evenings. I was hoping that if I denied it, the spirits would stop visiting me. So I thought. I thought I had shrugged the whole thing off, until one night on the way home, my friend, Gerry, asked me about a pin on my robe. Then, we talked about the pin and what it meant to me. I told her about seeing spirits that had crossed over to the white light. Gerry was very interested for a deep reason. She asked because her husband had passed away a year prior. I think we were meant to meet and find each other. I felt that she needed to talk to me. A spirit was pushing me to let her know something. I told my father there was an unbelievable thing going on with me. As long as it was from the highest and the best (God), I had to trust what was going on and not question it.

When I continued to go on Tuesday night to the Spiritualist Church, I was a watcher, not a medium. At the time, I did not know what a medium was. Once I learned that I was gifted (people who past away could communicate with me), I did not want people from my Roman Catholic Church to know. Within three months time of starting all of this, I began to question my ways. I drifted from the Spiritualist Church. I was questioning and thinking what would people be thinking of me because I was seeing spirits; some people do not understand mediumship. I kept asking myself, "What is going on with me?" I didn't want this gift; I didn't ask for it.

One night, after choir practice, Gerry gave me a ride home, and we talked. I told her that there was the presence of a man with us. I described the man the best I could. Gerry said that it was not her husband, Larry, but Jack, her brother-in-law. Gerry asked me if it was okay to tell Larry, and I said most certainly, yes.

Jack Shea was a six-foot-three man with brown hair, brown eyes, and a very kind heart. One morning, at about 6:25, he showed me some things. I saw the shadow of a little dog, a Scottie dog, followed by a flash of light. Gerry said it was Jack's dog, and she was not surprised they were together because they were like brothers on this side of life.

One day, when I was home praying my Rosary, I kept seeing a bird, and then, I got a message from Jack. He showed me, in some way, that he liked to read a special book. This made sense to Larry who was very good in the choir. The night before, at Mass, during a time of quiet reflection, Larry showed me a wooden cross, which had belonged to his mother. On December 20, Jack had a message of courage for Larry. Jack is someone special on the other side, and he sees what is going on.

On another day, in January, as I was praying the Rosary, I saw a starfish. It was brown, and it disappeared. I called Gerry to see if she knew what that meant, and she could not explain it. So, that following Sunday, I asked Larry. He replied that when he was a little boy, one of the things he did was try to save a brown starfish, just like the one Jack had shown me in my vision. I gave Gerry all the information so that she could tell Larry. Then, I said good night to Gerry. I went inside, and Chuck was watching the hockey game. Chuck looked at me strangely as I walked in the door. He asked, "Karen, what's the matter with you?" I said that I had a feeling I would think of while I was in the circle. Chuck said that the only way to find out is to go in. With a big, deep breath and my head up high, I started the new journey that would change my life. I knew that things would never be the same again. Tim and Will were happy to see me back in class.

Now, things were going to start up. The lights in the house started doing strange things, and I started seeing shapes of colors, flowers, and musical lyrics. I said to myself, "I'm in for a wild bus ride in my life."

Chuck said, "I told you, when you are ready, you would be going back to the Spiritualist Church."

So, when I went to Mass on Sunday, Gerry approached me. She said, "All the information I told her about Jack was true. Larry had told her so." This was the small push to send me back to classes on Tuesday night at the Spiritualist Church. I had to call Maria, the teacher at the Spiritualist Church, and ask her if it would be okay to come to classes again. Maria was quiet for a few minutes, and then, she said it was all right to come back to the circle. Chuck took me over, though I was nervous. I was thinking of the other students and if they would accept me back at my development class. When I was in the circle, I could see colors lighting up near the students; I could see the outlines of spirits. I also started seeing symbols. What I mean by symbols are possessions people had, such as a cat, dog, metals, jewels, or flowers. I'm a clairsentient and clairvoyant medium.

At the end of the class, my teacher asked if anyone was seeing, feeling, or smelling anything. I felt funny coming forward and say that I saw bright colors and an outline of something. The teacher told me that this was a good thing. The Roman Catholic feeling kept haunting me, making me feel funny. I felt as though my family might think I had gone crazy. So, I didn't tell my family for the longest time. When Mother's Day came, I finally came forward and told my father what was going on with me. I was in shock when my father told me not to question my gifts. "Just accept the gifts that God has given you." I decided to become a spiritualist!

Through my development classes, I learned where spiritualism began. Spiritualism was founded in Hydesville, New York in 1848 by the three Fox sisters. While living in a cottage, the Fox sisters began communicating with the so-called dead. The sisters heard rapping and footsteps. They also heard clapping, and they clapped back to communicate. It turned out to be a vagrant who was murdered in the house. The victim identified himself as Charles B. Rosna, and he successfully described his murder to Margaretta and Kate Fox and many witnesses. This proved to them and others the continuity of life after death since they later found Rosna's skeleton and belongings hidden behind a wall in the cottage. From that moment on, the Fox sisters became very famous, and that brought about the popularity of modern spiritualism.

Chapter Eleven
The Voice in the Night

When I was developing as a student medium, I would, on occasion, wake up in the middle of the night. Of course, sometimes, I did not always know what I would be seeing, hearing, or smelling.

One night, in 2001, I woke up, and I heard a man's voice say in a very soft tone, "Don't give up. Don't give up." I felt like the man was very tall but soft spoken. So, like always, I did not say anything to anyone. But after the kids went off to school, something pushed me to call my aunt, Ann Marie. I felt a little sorry sharing with her something she did not know. I was studying mediumship at the time, and I finally got enough courage to talk to her.

I said, "Auntie, you are going to think what I am going to tell you is kind of strange, but I have to tell you. Last night, at about 2:30 in the morning, I woke up. There was a tall man in the room. I could feel him. He said, 'Don't give up,' which did not make any sense to me."

She said, "Karen, you are describing my father. He had a soft-spoken voice and was tall." I did not know my grandfather very well. He crossed over before I was even born. She said that last night, she got up at about 2:30 in the morning and was feeling very sick. So, then, I told her the message again. She said thank you because that message was for her. I said okay, and I was happy that the message made her feel better. A relieved feeling came over me, and it was like the feeling that the messenger had for my aunt. My grandfather was a very kind and gentle man, and he was watching over my aunt.

"Auntie, I want to thank you for sharing his story with me, especially when I did not even know him," I told my aunt. When I first started on my spiritual journey, the other side would wake me up early in the morning. Well, I learned that was one thing the other side does. It wakes you up when you are sound asleep.

One night, when I was watching TV, and everyone was out of the house, my husband went out and picked up my daughter, Melissa, from dance class, and my son, Paul, went along for the ride. All was quiet, and the baby had gone to sleep early. All at once, I heard this voice say, "Karen." It was a voice I had heard before. It was my uncle, Larry, and all he said was my name. It was almost the one-year anniversary of his death. I said, "Uncle Larry, can you go to Auntie Eleanor and let her know that you are around her?" This made me start to think. There is really more, after we pass away.

The next day came, and the phone rang; it was Aunt Eleanor on the phone. She said, "Karen, remember how you have been telling me about what was going on with you; how you know that Uncle Larry is in a good place and not sick anymore?" I said yes. Well, the night before, at about 2:30 in the morning, she woke up and heard a voice say her name; that voice made her happy and feel a lot better. It was important for her to know that he was watching over her. She did not hear anything else, but that was all she needed to hear from him. Hearing from him made her feel at peace. My uncle, Larry, was not a very tall man, but in my eyes, he was very big.

There was one other time when I heard a voice again, and it said, "Karen." I knew the voice. It was Uncle Charlie. He said my name, letting me know he was around me and watching over me. I never told anyone I heard from Uncle Charlie. I kept it to myself.

Chapter Twelve

Sending Healing

When I went to choir practice on Wednesday night, one of the choir members was upset because her friend was diagnosed with cancer. We all got together in a circle and began to pray for Margaret's friend. When we were all done, I went over to Margaret and said, "When I go home, I am going to pray the Rosary for your friend." I felt like she needed extra prayers, and that is one thing we can all give, prayer. Sometimes, I do not feel like we give enough, or maybe, we just get too busy with our lives.

After Gerry dropped me off, I said hello, went upstairs, and made sure all the kids were asleep. Then, I went into my room and closed my bedroom door. Being alone is how I like to be during the time when I am saying my prayers. I asked that nothing but the highest and the best be around me. I asked that the Blessed Mother go to Kathy and let her feel her warmth and love as the Rosary was being prayed. There are different ways to send healing. This is one way that I like because of my Catholic spiritual beliefs.

After I was done, I went to sleep. Afterward, I was busy with my week according to the needs of my house. The next week came, and we went to choir practice. I went out with the choir for Chinese food. Margaret said she had some things to say. She said that Kathy, her friend with cancer, wanted to thank everybody for the prayers. After she was done, she sat down next to me and said she would like to thank me, especially. Her friend could sense a presence in the room with her, and the presence was comforting. I told Margaret that it was not me; it was those on the other side. I was just the instrument. We all have the ability to send healing. There are all kinds of healing, like I have mentioned. I was happy to hear that they were watching over Margaret's friend, and her friend knew that she was not alone. I would like to thank Margaret and her friend for sharing the stories about healing.

Chapter Thirteen

50th Anniversary Party for Mom and Dad

Sometimes, people who passed away come to me in my dreams. This happened about six years ago, when we were getting ready to have an anniversary party for my mother and father. My mother and father did all the planning themselves.

I went to bed one night, about three months before the party. I was having the same dream every night, and I did not understand it. I was in a very beautiful church, and there were friends there, except for one thing: these friends had already crossed over. One friend was my very best friend who I spoke about in this book. The other was someone I had not seen since I was a teen. Their names were Barry and Jeannie, and I knew them from my youth. We used to go fishing together. Barry passed away when he was a young man. They took me inside this church, which did not make any sense to me. Over to the side was a statue of a little flower. I thought, *Okay, it was nice of them to show me these things.*

Every night, it would be the same dream, but sometimes, they would show me more things in the church. They were trying to tell me something. They knew what was going to happen. The day of my parent's 50th anniversary party came. My husband and I dropped off the children and headed to the church. When we arrived at the church and I went inside, I could not believe what I was seeing. Over to the side was a statue of the little flower and some other things that had been shown to me. As I got talking to one of my folks' friends, St. Theresa appeared behind them. It took me off guard that everything from my dream was coming to be true. I know that this was their way of saying that they were with me, and that it was a very happy time. I came to know this a couple of years later, when people came to us through dreams. It was not until later that I learned that visions from the other side could come to you in dreams. This is called a visit or visitation.

Chapter Fourteen

My Grandmother's Family Secrets

During my spiritual journey, I began wondering if any of my family members had been a physic child or a medium. I knew I could not go to my mother because she was not enlightened at all. So, I thought about asking my aunt, Ann Marie, because she was very open. Well, as it turns out, there *was* someone who was a psychic—my grandmother. Let me tell you a little about my grandmother. She grew up in East Boston, Massachusetts. She was from a big family. Then, eventually, she married a man from East Boston. She had a black house and eight children all together. One night, she had a dream about my uncle, John. It was during the Korean War. She saw his jacket and his boots wet and knew something was wrong. Because she could not sleep, and did not sleep the rest of the night, she called my aunt, Tess, the following morning. She told her about her dream, and that she thought that Uncle John was in trouble. Later on, the phone rang, and it was the Navy calling. The officer told my grandmother that Uncle John's ship had tipped in the water, but everyone on the ship was okay. So, that was a big relief to her. There was another thing my aunt told me. My grandmother always paid attention to her dreams. That was something though because my grandmother was a very strict Irish Catholic, but she did possess psychic ability. It was something because, while growing up, my grandmother always gave me all religious things when I went to visit her. None of the other kids got religious gifts, except for me. One time, she gave me an old box full of coins that were worth something. I still have those old coins. She told me a story about how she earned the money.

As my aunt and I were talking, it came up in the conversation that my grandmother also had a special gift. This made me feel more at ease with my own gifts, and it tells me that I am not alone on my spiritual journey.

I told my aunt about seeing an aqua-green diamond ring and a pink outline of a dress. My aunt said that my grandmother was burned in a pink dress, and that she had the diamond ring that I had described. My aunt was very surprised to hear me describe things that I couldn't have known. Things began to connect. My aunt couldn't believe that I knew about the ring; this was so shocking to her. My aunt asked me if I talked to my mother about this. I said no. Then, my aunt began to tell me a story about my grandmother when she was in the hospital on her deathbed. My grandmother said that their Uncle Don, Aunt Tess, and her husband, all had passed away earlier. No one else could see them but her. My aunt dismissed this as a dying woman seeing things. Now, with what I have been going through, my aunt finally understood what her mother was seeing. The time was in the early 70s, when people weren't as open to mediumship.

Chapter Fifteen

Cliff's House

One night, I was at home and was getting ready to go to Cliff's house. He was a friend of Will's, and I had never met him. I was going to do readings for several people. I sat on the couch for a moment of silence. I looked up near my stairway, and I saw a picture frame. The frame was gold with black in the background. Then, it just disappeared. In its place was the spirit of a person, who began telling me how he was very humorous. I knew it had to be for Cliff. He told me how he looked, so Cliff would understand the information. Then, I went to take a shower, and while in the shower, I saw a medical seal and how his name was Henry. I said, "Thank goodness, it is the other side that sees me." I needed some privacy while I had my shower. So, I asked them if they could please wait until later. It was Saturday night, and I needed to get ready because I knew I would be picked up soon.

When we arrived, Will asked me if Lorie could go first, but they (meaning, the spirits) really wanted to see Cliff first. But I said okay. I had a feeling that the reading was not going to go well. Sure enough, it didn't—because the other people wanted to go first, too. Will said, "I think I understand the information that was coming through." But everything was still getting all jumbled up, and Lorie thought she could understand some things. Needless to say, the whole reading did not go as we expected. Yes, even mediums can have a bad day. Finally, I looked at Will and said, "Can I please see Cliff next? These two men have been with me since last night, and these two men have a lot to say." When Cliff came in and sat down, boy, all the information about Harry and Henry came out and made sense. He got off the table, went, and got a big picture he had on the wall. It was a big picture of Henry, who was a stand-up comic back in his day. The information was starting to be confirmed. Then, I told him about the doctor. Harry and I told him that his house was finally calming down. Cliff told me afterward how the house had not been calm for quite a while. I would like to thank Henry and Harry in spirit for sharing their stories and a special thank you to Cliff for letting me share their stories in this book.

One thing I did learn that summer night, in August 2002, is that whoever is going to come through is going to come through. Sometimes, I have to ask the others nicely if they could please let other people speak. Every now and then, a message will come that you need to deliver to another person. Now and again, people have a reading, expecting certain spirits to come through, but they don't. Other spirits came through instead because they wanted to let people know they were okay, too.

Chapter Sixteen

The Rosary

One thing I do before I do any readings is ask for special guidance by praying the Rosary. To me, praying the Rosary has always been a special prayer. I have always prayed to the Rosary my whole life, but I prayed to the Rosary more and learned about it more when I was in the convent. I always ask the Blessed Mother for special guidance. One time, I can remember praying to the Rosary, and all at once, I started seeing things outside my head. And it wouldn't be until later on that things made sense to me. It was all part of a learning process for me during my spiritual journey. I began to make a lot more sense of the symbols I was seeing; most of the time, they would be things that were relative to the person who was there in spirit or the person I was giving a reading to. I also learned how to trust, as long as it was from the highest and the best. The Blessed Mother has always been one of my special guides. We all have our own special people we like to help us along our journey.

When the other side started showing me things, it was when I started praying the Rosary. At first, I would do a double take. These are some of my experiences. With you, I am always saying how we all have our favorite prayer. Well, praying the Rosary was always one of my favorite prayers. Ever since the convent, I have always prayed the Rosary, especially before I do mediumship. The Blessed Mother is someone whom I go to for special guidance. Sometimes, I would ask Uncle Charlie and Uncle Larry, who had crossed over to the light; it is hard being a Roman Catholic with spiritualist gifts. But everyone has a gift; we all do things in different ways. One day, when I was out on my back porch praying the Rosary, I looked over to the right-hand side and saw a red rose outside my mind's eye. Then, it continued. Then, as I was praying my rosary, in front of me would be a blue rosary, and then, it would just disappear. One time, I can remember a special story that I would like to share.

Chapter Seventeen
Healing at the Hospital

I would like to share my experience when I was in the hospital. While I was growing up, I was nearly deaf in my left year. One time, I said to a friend that my right ear does not stop ringing, and she gave me the name of a very good ear doctor. I paid a visit to this doctor, and he really did not say anything other than some people just have ringing in their ears. He then looked into my left ear and asked if I would like to hear better out of that ear. I told him I would like that. Then, another doctor came in and said, "Let's see what we can do for you." I then went for several tests and later returned to the ear doctor. After he reviewed the test, he said he could help me. Although I was very surprised, I was happy and accepted his offer.

The day of the surgery came, and I ended up staying overnight in the hospital. I remember my husband thinking it was funny that the only place the hospital could find a bed for me was in the children's ward. I remember really wanting to go home, but I was sick. It was about 4 A.M. when I felt better and drifted into a much-needed sleep. About 5:30 A.M., I woke up, and at the foot of my bed was a big, almost clear-blue, ball of energy. I felt as if someone was there, and it was a very loving feeling, but it quickly went away.

After a couple of weeks, I went back to the doctor's office. After a few ear tests, he told me that I had 50 percent more hearing in that ear. I thanked him for providing me with this gift and for healing me. I knew then that the visitor in my room that night was an angel.

I also had to return to the hospital to have my sinuses operated on. Once I returned to the hospital, I could see the different colors of energies in the room, blue and green twinkling lights. The nurse came to get me to have my blood pressure taken, and as we talked, I could smell flowers, but there wasn't a flower in sight. I could see someone there with me who had crossed over.

Then, I went upstairs to the neurologist who was very nice. We were talking, and I told him how I was hearing impaired in my left ear, but after I had surgery, I could hear better. I told him how, over the summer, I could hear people talking through the windows; hear the leaves on the trees falling, the wind blowing, and the rain over the windows for the very first time. He looked at me and said, "What a wonderful story to share with people." I did not share my experiences with the angels or with people who had crossed over because I did not know him, but he was very interested in the healing process that went on with my ear.

One thing I do during healing work is ask all the guides for their help. If someone is going in for surgery, I ask the guides and angels to go with them and guide the doctor's hands while performing the surgery.

Chapter Eighteen
The Other Side at the Holidays

Going back to Christmas of 2001, I remember the weatherman saying it was going to be a windy and snowy winter, but all was calm that Christmas morning. I got up before everyone else and went downstairs. I went out to the enclosed back porch and put on some Christmas music. I went into the kitchen to put the lights on. Then, I woke up the entire house, and I had to say that I liked that idea since they never let my husband and I sleep in the morning, not even until 8:00 A.M. Someone always wakes us up. I put the music on a little louder so the family would wake up and come down the stairs to open their presents. Even my husband, who is the biggest kid of all, rushed down the stairs.

We all went into the kitchen to have breakfast. During breakfast, we gave each of the kids something small to open. Then, it happened. All the electricity in the house went out. Of course, the music went off, too. My daughter, Melissa, looked over at me as if I had done something to cause the lights to go out. I said, "Why are you looking at me? I didn't do anything."

Melissa is very aware of the other side, thus, she said, "Mommy, do you think the others are trying to tell us something?" Melissa was only five years old at the time. Then, I looked up and said that I would like to wish everyone on the other side, especially my family, a very Merry Christmas and a Happy New Year. All at once, all of the electricity came back on; even the music began playing where it left off, without anyone adjusting it. Then, there was absolute silence in the entire house. Not a sound was heard, except for the Christmas music. The other side loves to manipulate electricity. They often give us signs and communicate with us in this way.

Many other things have happened since that Christmas, but I realized that the spirit world still likes to be a part of our holidays and everyday life, if only to let us know that they are around. It was as if for one second, we were all united as one in silence, aware of each other's existence.

Even now, when I go to my development class on Tuesday nights, the lights blink off and on, as if to tell us they agree with what we perceive or they are present in our circle. The lights have also blinked dramatically, as if to say they really agree with what we are saying. This happens so often and consistently during our metaphysical work that it could never be discounted as coincidence. During Sunday services, the music from the portable stereo abruptly stops and changes to something else. Everyone knows it is the other side playing with us to let us know they are around. We laugh and acknowledge them, and then, we go about our business. It is so interesting and enjoyable to have this happen.

My daughter reminded me that spirits also play with toys. It was Christmas time (2004); my daughter received a rabbit that would sing "Somebody Loves You." You press his head to make him sing. The rabbit is up in the children's bedroom, and every so often, it begins to sing by itself. First, it sings "Somebody Loves You," and then, it sings "In Your Easter Bonnet." No one is there to press on the bunny's head; it just goes off automatically. I noticed this happened after my sister, Joanne, passed away. Melissa asked me if maybe it was Joanne trying to communicate with us. I said that yes, it was her way of saying hello; her way of saying, I am still present in your lives. These are a few ways that the other side lets us know that they are around, sending us love and reassurance that they are all right.

Chapter Nineteen
Medium's Day

During my spiritual journey with the other side, a number of things happened. I was invited to do Medium's Day at the Spiritualist Church. This is a place where people come to meet with a medium and request a reading. During the week, some people started coming to visit me, although they did not visit me during a party that a friend of mine had. I was surprised, but when I was doing the reading, a lot of people came. When Friday came, the day before Medium's Day, I looked out my window. On the right and on the left side, there were clouds, and my body felt funny. I said it was going to do something. I could feel it in my body. My friend, Sandy, called and said that she felt something like snow. I did not want to say anything at first, but deep down, I knew she was right, and I was a little disappointed. But everything happens for a reason. It was near the end of another year. That night, the biggest snowstorm hit for that year. Once again, I said everything happens for a reason. It was kind of funny because one of my guides in spirit is Uncle Larry. He told me to have patience for the first couple of weeks, given that it was time to move forward. Needless to say, it kept snowing and snowing. Before I went to sleep, I said my prayers. Then, I went to sleep. The next morning, my phone rang. It was another friend. She asked if Medium's Day was still on. I responded that I did not know, but I would find out. Too bad, the other side does not let you know whether it is there or not. So, I tried my teacher's house. She was not home, so I called the church. Sure enough, it was cancelled due to the storm.

My friend called back and said okay. She had people coming from Boston. There was something about what she said earlier. The other side does not let you know because the people who have crossed over were also quiet. Later on that day, they started letting me know they were around me. They started showing me things, like a German shepherd. And my friend, Sandy, called. As we were talking on the phone, the bedroom light started blinking on and off. Then, Sandy's light started blinking at her home. She did say one thing about her father who started coming through. When he started coming through, he said his age. I told Sandy that his age was fifty years when he passed. She said yes, and with that, our light went off, and we both chuckled, for her father had a lot to say. So, the reading went on. He told me that he had dark-brown hair, brown eyes, and a dog, and Sandy said yes. I asked her if she has a dog over in the spirit world, and she said yes. Then, I asked her if the dog was German shepherd, and she said yes. There were a couple of other things that were private. And she validated everything. I would like to thank Sandy, and even her German shepherd, for sharing her story with me.

A year later, another Medium's Day…

In March 2005, I got invited again to participate in Medium's Day. A reading is when someone, from any walk of life, comes to the church to receive a message from someone who had crossed over to the other side.

The night before, I was watching the news on TV, and a northeaster was predicted; last year, a snowstorm, and this year, a rainstorm. They were also saying that it was going to be really windy and wild outside. Then, I got to thinking about how Medium's Day was cancelled last year with the snowstorm, hoping it wouldn't be cancelled again this year. When it was time for me to go upstairs to bed, I thought, whatever will be will be. If Medium's Day was cancelled, then it wasn't meant to be. I said some prayers and asked my guides and angels to keep me and my family safe. Then, I drifted off to sleep. During the night, I was awakened by the sounds of the wild wind. Then, I got to thinking about Medium's Day again. The next morning came, and I went down to make the kids' breakfast, thinking I would get a phone call that Medium's Day had been cancelled. When the phone didn't ring, I went upstairs to take my shower. After my shower, in my bedroom, I said some special prayers and asked that no lower energies come in (meaning, only those of positive influence and light would be welcomed). Then, Chuck and I packed up all the kids, drove to the church, and said my good-byes to Chuck and the kids when we reached the church, and in I went. Reverend (Rev.) Marie was there, waiting at the door for me.

"Thank goodness, you showed up; someone couldn't make it because of the weather," she said. Then, I went upstairs and saw that my favorite table was available. It is my favorite because I feel drawn to the good energy in that area. When Rev. Marie went down to get a client, I saw a myriad of orbs dancing by the piano. Orbs are spirit energies. The client came upstairs; the platform was dancing in orbs, too. When I was finished with the client's reading, Rev. Marie told me that I could have a break. I went back downstairs and told Marie it would be fun to have a reading, too. She asked Liam if he would give me a reading, to which he agreed. When we sat down up in the church, all the orbs were still present. After Liam was done with the reading, he asked me for one. I also agreed. Halfway through the reading, the winds calmed down, and the sun began to come out. In the back of the church, there was an empty table, where earlier, someone had been doing readings. All at once, we heard a pencil drop. Liam and I just looked at each other. Even mediums can be caught off guard! Liam and I egged each other on, until I went over to the table to investigate. When I approached the table, there was no pencil there. I told Liam there wasn't a pencil. We just looked at each other and said that even though no one was there, the spirits were still looking to be heard. We were both quite surprised. The best thing about this clairaudient experience is that we shared it and could validate the experience for each other.

Chapter Twenty
At the Workshop

I can remember going to a workshop at the Spiritualist Church in October 2003. One of the mediums came over from England. As the medium was talking, the air started lighting up with different colors: blue, green, yellow, and purple. I looked over by the piano, and behind the flowers, I saw a little boy. The boy was about twelve years old, with short brown hair and brown eyes. I asked him if he was with someone. We communicated telepathically, as is usual with spirits. He told me that he was not alone, and that he was with his friend. His friend had dark, wavy brown hair, dark-brown eyes, and was one year younger. During the night, he kept popping his head in and out, but he did not come closer. I knew that he was shy. I didn't say anything to anyone about him, but when we had our Tuesday night class, I saw him come in the room. Something told me to ask Tim. So, when Tim came over, I started talking to him about the little boy behind the flower at the workshop and how he was with his friend. Tim told me that before the church was a Spiritualist Church, it was a Baptist Church, and they used to teach Sunday school. He said, "I have something to show you downstairs after class." When class ended, Tim took me downstairs and we went over to this very old picture. It was dated 1738. When I looked at the picture, I saw the boy who was behind the flowers. Then, another feeling came over me. When I looked at the middle of the picture, there was his friend. After that, we went upstairs.
I said to Marie, "I am never going to question the other side again."

During the workshop, I learned to ask the children who they were with. This was one thing I was glad to learn because there were children who had crossed over at my house; it never dawned on me to ask them who they were with because they get busy giving messages to their family and friends.

Chapter Twenty-One

Seeing Johnny

Johnny's story is very special because he passed away at a very young age. I did not know him, so everything you will hear is through others who knew Johnny. I did not know him physically, but I knew him spiritually.

One morning, I woke up about 6:15 A.M., and everything was nice and peaceful. All at once, I saw a green turtle on the wall, and something said to me, *"Turtle on the loose."* So, I wrote the message down. It did not make sense to me; there were three names along with the information: David, Danny, and Donny. They were all alive. My husband validated some of the information, so I called his brother, Bob, for more corroboration. He understood. My brother-in-law, Johnny, had passed away when he was only twelve, and it was a great loss to the family. I really never knew Johnny, and the family did not really talk about him. I never asked Chuck about him. So, Bob told me that when he was a teenager, he had had two turtles. Bob told me a story about how his turtles were missing for two days. Bob had thought that it was Chuck who had taken them. Come to think of it, it was Jimmy and Johnny. Johnny was a twin, and Jimmy was the surviving brother. Then, I asked Bob about the three names that Johnny had given me and told me that they were friends of Johnny's.

When I finished on the phone, the strangest thing happened. Bob called back and told me that when we finished talking, Jimmy called, and Bob gave him the information. The information made Jimmy happy. All was quiet for about a year. One night, when I was in my development class, we were all giving messages back and forth to each other. I can remember looking over at my friend, Mike. There was a young boy behind him, but I could not make him out. All I could see was the color of his eyes, which were very white and dazzling; he stayed with Mike for a couple of minutes. Then, with the drop of a dime, he just disappeared. We all said a blessing, and class was over. We were all talking in the car. Phyllis was driving, and I got to thinking that I should have told Mike about the boy. Phyllis got ready to pull into my driveway, and I jumped. I saw a boy, about twelve years old, with a dark-blue jacket, a white shirt, and a horizontal striped tie. I really wanted to say, "Phyllis, watch out for the boy in the driveway."

Before he disappeared, the boy said, "Call the house and check on Papa." I did not tell anyone. We usually talk for a while before I go in the house, but this time, I did not. Then, I said that I should have told Mike about the boy. So, I called Mike the next day and told him about the twelve-year-old boy whom I saw behind him. He did not understand, but suggested I ask some of the others. I did, but they did not understand the boy either. Finally, Chuck came home, and I asked him if he knew who the boy was. I gave him all the information about him. There was dead silence, like I had hit a nerve.

Chuck was not being much help, so I called Bob. I told Bob about the boy in my driveway—what he looked like and what he was wearing. Bob got quiet on the phone. I said, "This poor little boy does not belong to anyone."

Then, Bob said, "Karen, that was my brother, Johnny." I was surprised; Chuck had never told me how Johnny had passed. Johnny had a closed casket because of the damage from the car accident, and Bob and his papa were the only ones who saw Johnny at the hospital. Bob validated the clothing he had on. After all that Bob told me, I got off the phone and looked over at Chuck. You see, my husband was one of the last people in his family to see his brother alive. He then told me how he told Johnny not to cross on the busy highway because he would get killed. It was less than two minutes later that he was hit and killed. It was a very bad accident, and it was not the driver's fault. It was just bad judgment on Johnny's part. Then, I went to bed, but I forgot to give Bob the message. So, the next morning, I called him up. I talked to Ritchie and mentioned how Johnny was saying that there was something wrong with Papa, and sure enough, there was. The asthma was getting worse. So, I said, "Please let Bob know that Johnny is watching over Papa." The other side does watch over us, and they do have ways of letting us know.

I just want to share one more thing. The next day, Jimmy came over to the house. Chuck and Jimmy were going to see the Bruins play. I told Jimmy about Johnny, and he told me how he and Johnny let the turtles out. Then, my husband, who does not understand mediumship, finally said, "I got blamed for that."

As they were getting ready and were going to go out the door, I said, "Boys, by the way, Johnny says the Bruins are going to lose, and they are going to lose bad." Well, at about 9:00 P.M., I put on the hockey game, and the sports commentator came on and said he had not seen anything like it in a long time; the Bruins got blown away in their own building. I would like to thank my brother-in-law for sharing his story with me and letting me know that, even though I did not know him physically, I know him through spirit.

Chapter Twenty-Two

Jerry Shea

What can I say? For a long time, Jerry Shea did not have any messages for his wife, Gerry. I explained to Gerry that whoever is supposed to come through will come through. Gerry is very open to mediumship. When Gerry would ask me about him, sometimes, there were messages for other people. Little did she know that she would be the medium for "the medium."

One night, I was at home, and I started to have difficulty breathing, but then, the feeling passed. Later, I learned it was how Jerry felt as he had a heart attack and passed away. Jerry started coming through. When Jerry came for a visit, he made my hands very sore. So, I asked his wife if Jerry had sore hands, and she said yes. I asked if there was a red and white flower that he always liked when he was alive. Then, he told me to say the number five three times. Gerry said, yes, there were three sets of five in the family. Then, he said the name Mo. That was their daughter, and that was his way of letting Gerry know that he was around. Then, he showed me a cupcake. I proceeded to tell Gerry what I saw, and she knew right away. After the reading was done, she told me how her daughter was talking about having cupcakes at her wedding the other day. I told her that he must be listening because he knew what they were saying and planning. There was one more thing that Jerry said to Gerry before he was done. That was to remind her how he used to sneak down to the refrigerator late at night for something sweet. His left hand used to be sore, but it was not sore anymore. He also wanted her to have white roses at the wedding because white roses mean congratulations. Gerry later told me that, at Mo's wedding, they had placed two white roses on the altar; they knew that he would be there spiritually for the two of them.

Chapter Twenty-Three
Tim's Friend

One night, after class, my friend, Tim, was taking me home, and we were enjoying a light conversation while he was driving. After Tim dropped me off at home, I was doing something in the kitchen, and I happened to come across one of the children's plain, white pieces of paper used for coloring. As I was picking the pieces up, a man's face manifested on one of them. He had curly hair, a mustache, and a pale complexion. He told me to tell Tim he was with him. Then, as suddenly as he had appeared, he disappeared. I wasn't sure what it all meant. The next day, I gave Tim a call to tell him what I had seen and gave him the message. Tim was very happy that I told him that because he knew who the person was.

Chapter Twenty-Four

Blessing From the Other Side
(In Loving Memory of Joanne)

One morning, I got up and went downstairs. Before everyone got up, I went in the kitchen, and the strangest thing happened. I looked at the refrigerator, and it had a lot of photographs on it, but when I looked on the floor, there was my sister's picture. It had had a pretty good magnet on it because it was bigger than some of the other photos. So, I thought that was kind of strange. I said, "Joanne, what are you doing on the kitchen floor?" So, I put her back where she belonged, and I went on with my day, getting the children off to school and cleaning the house. Well, later on that day, we went to church with the kids, and when we got home, the phone rang, and it was my mother. She asked me to get Chuck on the phone. So, I told Chuck that my mother wanted to speak to him. When he got off the phone, he said, "Karen and Missey, come down here now." I did not understand why he was so upset. He said, "I have some sad news to tell you. Your sister has passed away." I was surprised to hear the news. Then, I thought of the photograph on the refrigerator and told Chuck and the kids about it.

Then, I said, "My goodness, she was letting me know ahead of time." We had to wait two weeks before she could come home for her services because she lived in Jamaica, and there were many legal things that we had to go through. Well, the weekend finally came, and my father came to get me, and we went to the service. I told my father the story about the photo, and he told me a couple of stories about my sister. I said, "Dad, I think she knew she was going to cross over." And then, there was silence.

In the car, he said, "Karen, you know her friend down in Jamaica said the same thing…that is something." I thought, *Nothing in life is coincidental*. When we got to the house, my mother told me how she had asked my cousin,

Stephen, to speak at the wake and share stories about my sister. I thought, well, I am not going to say anything. So, I went outside because it was a nice spring day. I said some prayers for my sister, who was learning and growing on the other side. When we went to the funeral parlor, there was no one there yet, and we went over to the casket and said some prayers. It was a closed casket, but there was a nice picture of my sister on top. When I looked up at the picture, it lit up in blue. I am a clairvoyant medium, and I see things outside my mind's eye that make me feel a lot better; I knew she was there spiritually. As the day went, I saw energy colors near some people I knew. I said to the people who knew my sister, "You know, she is around." They said they could feel her also, and that made them feel better. The priest finally came in, and the room was lighting up in all these different colors of blue and purple.

Well, after that, the priest said some prayers. He said, "Does anybody have something that they want to share?" My mother spoke, then my aunt spoke, and all at once, the room got very quiet. I was waiting for my cousin to speak, but he said nothing. I felt like something was pushing me out of the choir, and the next thing I knew, I was going up to speak, even though I was not scheduled to speak. Well, something pushed me right up there. I told them how my sister asked me a long time ago, "What happens to you after you die?" I never had an answer for her until the last time she was here, visiting, and I told her how I was training to be a medium. Now, I finally had an answer. I told her that when you leave the physical world, you leave your physical body. When you die, your family and friends who have gone before you are there to greet you on the other side, as guides. Angels take us up to meet God, and then, we learn and grow over there. After I was done, it was quiet for a minute. My mother said she had something else she would like to share and asked Steven if he was going to speak. But, he could not speak after the final prayers from the priest. The people and family members came over and said their condolences. Some of my cousins said they really loved what I said. It made me feel so much better, knowing that there is more to learn after we leave this world. When we got back to my mother's house, I saw my cousin, Steven, and asked him why he didn't speak. He hesitated and told me how he felt he couldn't speak and knew that I was supposed to.

My sister and I were very close. Of course, there were times we did not see eye to eye on things, but that is normal. When the day of the funeral came, my sister and I did readings from the Scripture. I thought mine was very good; the angels were in it. I felt that it was planned, but on the other hand, it was one of the hardest things I had to do. After I was done and the Mass was almost over, I looked up, and on the right-hand side, in front of the flowers, there was a big, white mist; it seemed like it was going up and leaving. I knew who it was. Since my sister died a year ago, she has let me know, on more than one occasion, that she is helping me when I do my mediumship. One thing I would like to say is, since my sister's passing, you always remember the loved ones you lost, but it is different, and if you are open, they will let you know that they are around.

Chapter Twenty-Five
In Memory of Jimmy Jackson

The day before we went to Uncle Jimmy's wake, everything was quiet and subdued. I had gone to a workshop the day before—a workshop strictly for mediums and meant to enrich one's self. This workshop was taught by an English medium, which for me was a very special treat for my growth and enlightenment. I am always trying to understand the gift God has given me. Throughout this book, you will hear me state that I have never wanted or asked for this gift, which frankly is the truth. I had never wanted this, but I have learned to accept and develop it. Before I knew it, the workshop was over, and the next day came, which was before Jimmy had passed away.

Finally, the day of the wake had come. My husband and I were getting ready; it was all pretty mundane and usual, nothing special yet. Being that it was Chuck's uncle who had passed on, he was unusually subdued. I proceeded to ask Chuck if he was all right, and he responded that he was fine. He was especially close to his deceased uncle. Not knowing much about Uncle Jimmy, I told Chuck that I believed that Jimmy had died of a broken heart, and this was because the love of his life had died just two months before. He looked at me and stated, "Karen, you are right." Quietly, I thought to myself, *What a nice way to cross over, just to drift off in your sleep, without the physical pain that occurs in everyday life*. Chuck knows and understands that mediumship is real. In one of the chapters of my book, I have spoken about electricity and how this is one way that the other side lets us know they are around. Let me share this other story with you, and also to let you know how the other side shows us things. When we got to the funeral parlor to pay our respects, I said to Chuck, "You know, he is not really there. He is over with his wife and son (who had already passed), learning and growing."

Chuck actually said, "I knew that when we went inside and we went over to the casket and paid our respects and said some prayers." Prayer always helps them over at the other side. While we were there, I saw all the nice family photos. Then, something happened that did not make any sense to me. I pay attention, and I see things that other people don't see. All at once, there were extra photos (they were only silhouettes) in the casket, and all of a sudden, they disappeared.

Chuck and I went over to his cousin, Tommy, and told him how sorry we felt. I did not say anything to Tommy about being a medium because I didn't think it was the right time. Feeling his sadness, I said, "Your father died of a broken heart." He agreed. Then, I said to him, "He is reunited with loved ones."

Tommy said, "Yes."

I said, "What a nice way to pass away, during his sleep."

Tommy replied, "Yes."

The last thing that I said was, "They are together over there, and they are happy."

And he said, "Yes." You see, we miss them more than they miss us because they can still see us. When we sat down, all at once, the lights right next to us started blinking on and off. It happened one more time.

Jennie said, "Karen, I have something to show you." She took out a photograph, and I could not believe my eyes. They were silhouettes, just like the ones I had seen earlier in the casket—during the time we said our prayers. It was most unreal because they were pictures of my mother-in-law and of my uncle. It just amazed me that so much energy came in so fast. Just before we left, it started lighting up in bluish color. We started to say our good-byes, and on the way home, I told Chuck how the spirits are always around us, even though they are not here physically. I would like to let Uncle Jimmy's spirit know that love never dies and is eternal.

Chapter Twenty-Six

Losing a Loved One

There are many books that talk about grief. There are two stories that really touched me. My cousin, Linda, who I never knew, was an adult and living on her own. She came from a family of seven. It was not easy for her family to lose Linda. She had cancer, just like her mother who had already passed away. I began to see symbols like balloons and monarch butterflies. I knew it had nothing to do with my sister, Joanne. After a while, I saw a pair of blue rosary beads. I decided to write these visions down because when these symbols appear, they come so fast and disappear in a blink of an eye.

When the day of my sister's wake came, and after everything was calm, I saw my cousin, Pattie, and I asked her to come to my mother's house. I had something interesting to tell her. I wasn't sure if she would be open to what I had to say, but I knew I had to tell her what I was seeing.

As the night went on, my uncle, Marty, started talking to my mother and I about losing his daughter. The way he talked about her really touched my heart. He looked over at my mother and said, "Betty, it's not easy to lose a child." Seeing the look on my uncle's face made me feel sad. It doesn't matter what age a child is. It is painful and heartbreaking to lose a child. As he continued to talk, I really listened to him. I realized how difficult it must have been for my father to travel to Jamaica to bring his daughter's body home. He had to go through many legal hassles and waited two weeks before finally being able to bring Joanne back to the family. It was a very long and sad two weeks for my father to deal with by himself. It seems very cruel for someone to have to go through these legal procedures with such intense grief. It's hard for a parent to endure grief for a child.

When Pattie came back to my mother's house after Joanne's funeral, she gathered her sisters and her father. We sat in a semicircle, and I told them about the information coming through their sister, Linda.

Patti remembered that Linda had a pair of blue rosary beads. In fact, Patti said that they were going to give her green beads instead, but in the end, Linda was given the blue rosary beads. Patti was surprised to hear this. Patti continued to identify objects and symbols that I had seen associated with her sister on the other side. I asked Pattie if there were balloons at Linda's funeral, and she said yes. Pattie also informed me that Linda loved Monarch butterflies—the other symbol that appeared.

I told my uncle and my cousins that Linda was around them, and that she was at peace.

In fact, Linda told me that her mother was also with her, along with others who had passed into the light. Everyone was very quiet. I felt that I could finally relax.

Then, I looked over and remembered what made me happy. I was happy that I could relay this message to my cousins and my uncle. They were open enough to accept this information and felt good about it. They were relieved to know Linda won her battle with cancer and was at peace at last! It seemed that Linda waited until her family was all together before she came to tell them of her continuing life. I was happy to be the messenger for her.

Sometimes, when someone is about to pass over, they wait until they are alone. Family members may be by their bedside for days, but as soon as they leave for a moment, the loved one may pass. Others may wait until everyone is present and accounted for before they pass to the other side. When they decide to leave, it is their own personal choice.

I can remember someone telling me about a man who was dying. His family members were all there, along with hospice members. Everyone was taking care of him and spending their time saying good-bye. No one wanted to leave the man's side in case something happened. As soon as the family left the room for a few minutes, the man passed away. It was almost as if he waited to die alone, without everyone there. Hence, you should never feel guilty if you are not present when your loved one dies. They may have planned it that way.

You can always say good-bye, even after your loved one passes over. They are usually listening in and giving you signs from the other side. They are available to help and guide you. At first, I felt bad about not seeing my sister before she passed. Her casket was closed because it took so long to get her body home. I never did get to see her and say my good-bye. I am a medium, but I am still a human being with feelings, and I missed my sister.

Then, Joanne started letting me know that she was around. She sends me messages and lets me know when she is present, when she is with me. It is very comforting to know that life goes on, and that love never dies. We are eternal!

This chapter is written in loving memory of my cousin, Linda, who I never knew in life but got to know spiritually. I also think of Uncle Marty, who made me realize that it is not easy to lose a child no matter what the age. Also, the man who was attended by hospice and his family helped me to know that you can have some say when you'll finally pass. I think hospice is a wonderful agency to help such ill people pass over to the other side with a bit of dignity.

When it is my time to cross over into the light, I hope my family and friends from both sides are there to help me pass in peace and dignity.

Chapter Twenty-Seven
Music

I have learned that music, during prayer or meditation, raises your vibration. It also adds a great sense of peace to your meditation or prayer, and this is also something nice to have on during a healing process.

One time, I use to sing in my church choir. One night, we were at practice, and we all started singing. All at once, the whole choir room began lighting up in these brilliant colors, and it seemed like whenever there was music on, no matter where I was, at home or at church, the other side would do their thing, but the brilliance in the energy and words cannot be described. One thing I have learned is that music brings up the vibration, just like when we pray for our family and friends who have crossed over; the light prayer to them is like music. It helps them with their learning and growing on the other side. One time, I can remember being at the choir practice, and John, my choir director, was going over and over the music with the altos. Whenever I would look down at the music, especially with certain songs, the other side would add extra musical lyrics, and this would make me smile. One time, one of the choir members said, "Karen, I can tell, sometimes, when you see things, your face changes." I told her about the building of the energies on the other side and how they enjoy the music.

One other time, I can remember something that happened at choir practice. I was upset, and John came over to me and said to me, "Karen, aren't we a sensitive group?" And that got me thinking. So, the next time I saw Marie, I said to her, "I am not sure about mediumship."

Then, she asked me, "Karen, "what's wrong?"

I said, "I am just too sensitive." And then, she told me how mediums are more sensitive than most people, and when she was telling me this, we had just finished listening to music, and the room was lighting up.

Chapter Twenty-Eight

Father Jay

During my spiritual journey, there have been some special people who have been part of my life.

One of the special people who have been part of my life is Father Jay, and I have known him for almost twenty-seven years. I have never known a time when he had not been there to help me.

Nothing in life is coincidental, but it always seemed as if Father Jay had been there whenever I really needed him.

When I was in the convent, I remember Father Jay being there for me until the nuns told me I had to see one of the priests if I wanted to talk to someone. That was one of the reasons I left the convent—because I knew I couldn't say good-bye to my friend. When things started happening to me, I didn't know where to turn. Things worsened before I knew there was a Spiritualist Church.

I could remember going to my own parish priest, but he didn't understand where I was coming from, and when I sat down to talk to him, he didn't understand.

When I was speaking to him, I was talking fast, and he had asked me if I was okay. Now, I know why I talked fast, and at that time, I didn't know all the answers either. When I was finished talking to him, I felt a little sad because I knew that Father Jay thought I had gone off the deep end.

But what bothered me the most was that, at the end of our talk, he asked me if I had any of the inside scoop about the lottery numbers. I told him that a spirit does not work that way. So, after our conversation, I thought that perhaps I shouldn't do anymore medium work and once again put it on the back burner.

But little did I know that spirits had more in store for me. One of my friends, Phyllis, told me, "Karen, I do not think you can get away from mediumship, and I think you know that."

I knew, deep down inside, that she was right. So, I knew there was one priest I could talk to, and that someone was Father Jay.

I picked up the phone and gave Father Jay a phone call. He wasn't there, so I left a message on his answering machine. I asked him to please call me when he had a chance.

A couple of weeks went by, and my parent's 50th anniversary came up. When we got to the church in Norwood, Massachusetts, Saint Joseph Worship had closed down with all the other church closings. I kind of avoided talking to them. Then, we went to the reception in Walpole at the Walpole Country Club.

I began thinking about my conversation with my own parish priest, and so, I started avoiding Father Jay because I didn't want him to think I had snapped my beanie altogether.

For a while, before we went inside the hall, I got to avoid Father Jay. I was talking to my cousin, Joe, who came from California, and I was also speaking to Steve.

Then, I told Chuck that I wasn't going to talk to Father Jay, Chuck looked very surprised at me. He then said, "Karen, you have been wanting to talk to him for a long time, and you have the chance to talk to him and explain to him what has been going on with you spiritually."

Then, I told Chuck that I just changed my mind, and that I was okay with everything that was going on with me. But deep down inside, I knew that I needed to tell him what was going on with me spiritually.

Just then, I went to turn around, and wouldn't you know it, after avoiding Father Jay for two hours and thinking I wouldn't have to speak to him, there he was. He looked at me and smiled. There he was with his caper skin, brown frock on, and what I would refer to as his Jesus sandals. He looked me right in the eyes and said to me, "Karen, have you been avoiding me? Whenever I wanted to talk to you, you would just disappear. It seemed like there has been a lot of that going on lately." I told Father Jay that I had been seeing people who had passed away and how they would just disappear.

I also told him of how upset I was when he didn't return my phone call, and that I didn't want him to think that I had gone off the deep end.

As we got talking, I told him what was going on with me, thinking that I would get the same reaction out of him that I got from my own parish priest.

Then, his friend who passed away from sudden death had some messages for Father Jay. His friend was a priest, also. Then again, Father Jay looked at me with that look on his face and told me he could understand the information from his friend.

After his reading was done, he validated all the information. He looked at me, smiled, and told me that I had a special gift from God, and that he didn't think I had gone off the deep end at all.

This would be the first time of many talks with Father Jay. Just last summer, on July 16, 2004, we went up to Maine. Chuck told me, "Karen, there is going to be a special surprise for you." I am the type of person who likes to be busy all the time, and I knew I was going to be bored stiff up there, but I knew Chuck and the kids liked it in Maine. So, I went to Maine anyway, but I almost stayed home.

After a couple of days, when we were all settled in, we went to the fair, and then, we all decided to go to the pool.

My son, Paul, started laughing at me on our way over to the pool, and kids being kids, looked at me and said, "Mommy, you are in trouble you know, for whatever it is you do when you leave the house with your friends on Tuesday nights. Someone on Brown Street is going to visit you."

Chuck looked at Paul and told him that he was going to ruin my surprise. So, I made off like I didn't hear him. It started getting late in the day, and I looked at Chuck just to play along with them and said to Paul, "I guess my surprise isn't here today. It will just have to wait."

One thing I have learned about Father Jay, after knowing him for so many years, is that the last laugh is always on him. As soon as I was done joking with Paul, he told me, with a big grin on his face, "Here is our surprise now, Mommy."

There was Father Jay with Mom and Dad. They had been talking to some of our relatives, and Father Jay came in the pool area and sat down with us. It is something how things work sometimes. Father Jay asked me how everything was going, and then talked to Chuck for a while. Then, Father Jay got back to me and asked me if I heard any more from my sister who had passed over into the white light on the other side. And I told him that she was quiet, that I hadn't heard from her for six moths after she passed. I told him how she must be busy learning and growing spiritually on the other side, in the white light. I told Father Jay that, usually, the messages are not for me but for other people.

He looked at me with that look on his face and asked me if I had any messages for him from anyone whom he had known over on the other side.

Chuck looked at me and told me that it was okay. Mom and Dad were over there, still talking to family members at the birthday party they were having.

I said, "Yes, there is a man next to you named Joseph." Father Jay looked at me. And Chuck told me to explain to him. "No, Father, there is a man next to you who was five seven, and his name was Joseph. He was sick before he passed away."

Father Jay said, "Yes, there was someone like that I had known."

I asked him, "Did your mother help him?" I didn't really know his mother. He said, "Yes."

As Father Jay's reading continued, I asked him, "Did your mother help people when she was alive?

He said, "Yes." After the rest of Father Jay's reading was finished and he had validated all the information, Mom and Dad came over. I smiled back at Father Jay, and he smiled back at me.

There was one more time when I talked to Father Jay on the phone. It was in the fall, and he told me, "Karen, do what you have to do. I know you will do the right thing in your life, and that God will always be there to guide you."

One thing I also remember about our trip to Maine it that someone my mother knew up there needed healing, and Father Jay did some healing on this person, and when he was done, he went on his way. Mother told us that when Father Jay was praying for that person, his hands became very hot. My mother, who isn't enlightened, said, "He is a healer."

I would like to give a very special thank you to Father Jay for believing in me, and I know he has always been one of my mentors. I am very proud to call him a friend, and I would like to say to him, "Father, it is nice to know that there are still some true priests out there, especially with the way things are today. Once again, Father Jay, thank you for sharing your stories and for always being there for me, even when my own parish priest was not there for me."

One thing I have learned and is that we are all gifted in our own way, and that we all have the gift to connect with the other side. It is just different for each person. This is one thing that Father Jay had made me realize when my mother told me about her friend and how Father Jay's hands got very warm.

To me, that is what mediumship is all about. It is about healing. I am just the middle person between the worlds, and that is what Father Jay made me and my friends at the Spiritualist Church in Quincy realize.

Chapter Twenty-Nine
Development

Below are some of my favorite exercises that I learned from my development classed taught by Reverend Marie. I would like to share them with you so you could use them if ever you wish to communicate with anyone living on the other side, in the white light. I mentioned my development circle in these exercises because that is where I learned to control what was going on when spirits wanted to communicate with me. I needed to know what to do with the way I was feeling things, seeing things, and also hearing things. I mentioned the Spiritualist Church in my book because that is the place that helped me to learn about mediumship. They taught me how to develop my gift more fully.

If you would like to find sources of information, a good place to look in a New Age bookstore. They often have classes that will help individuals learn how to speak to the other side. Or you can go to a Spiritualist Church like I did. It is your choice since you have the gift of free will in your life.

I hope you enjoy these exercises. I have used them, and they are some of my favorites. I want to share these experiences with you. Remember to always ask the white light for protection before using any of these exercises.

Chapter Thirty

Meditation

Here is a meditation I would like to share with you. If possible, start your music half an hour before meditating. You will find it makes a big difference in the energy. You can begin in any way that feels right to you. I usually light a candle (make sure it is safely placed away from children) and place my angel statue in the center. For your development, sit down in a quiet place.

Make an appointment every day if you cannot just mentally say, "I have something to do, and I will do it when I have time." If at anytime you feel like you are uncomfortable, you may try some other time. Sit in a straight chair with your legs uncrossed. Then, breathe in and out several times, in through the nose and out through the mouth, until you feel relaxed. Then, ask the white light to keep you safe and protected. Start from the top of your head, and then, slowly, go down through all your body parts, then, down to your toes and any part of your body you may have missed, until you are totally relaxed. Then, I usually ask the white light to be in the back of me, in the front of me, on the right side, and on the left side of me. Next, picture a church or some other Holy place where you feel comfortable. I usually picture a church, but it is your choice. I see the tallest trees with more bright, green leaves, and then, I go down along a path. The path is nice and sandy. I go along the path until I see a white church in front of me, and then, the sandy path turns into a marble path. Then, I see the doorway made of wood with shiny gold hinges. I open the door, and then I enter. As I continue to enter, I see a beautiful set of marble stairs going up to the sacred sanctuary. Ten steps lead up. I notice that each step has a flower on it, roses of all colors: red, pink, white, and yellow. When I get to the top of the stairs, I look and say some prayers. Then, I go in, and I look and notice some really nice stained glass windows with all the color of the rainbow in them. Then, I see some more stairs going up to a room. There are ten more stairs. On these stairs, there are beautiful crystals of each shade. When I get to the top and entered the room, I see some pillars that almost look like clouds. Then, I sit down and wait for someone from the other side to come and visit. As long as they are in the light, I look at them and see what they look like, what special things they did, what they wanted me to see, and how they died. When I meditate, my guides usually come in. They have been my spirit guides for as long as I can remember. My guides always tell me to look, listen, and speak after they are done. I say some prayers with them and thank them for coming. Then, I go back the same way I came in, and usually, my guides stay with me until I feel my feet underneath me. You can do the same if you wish, or you can do it on your own way. Then, bring yourself into your room, feel your feet underneath you, and when you feel ready, open your eyes.

Chapter Thirty-One
Writing a Letter to a Deceased Loved One

This is a special exercise that my friend, Gus, told me about when I lost my sister.

Take a piece of paper and a pencil in your hand. Write down all of your feelings to your loved one. Don't think they are not listening because they are very aware of what you are doing. When it was the day of my sister's wake, my daughter said that she didn't even get to say good-bye to her aunt, and then, I thought about what Gus told me. At first, I didn't think Melissa would have enough time to write the letter because my father was on his way to pick us up. Then, the strangest thing happened. The phone rang. It was my father, and he was running late. I turned my head up to heaven and thanked whoever sent us the extra time to write the letter. I called Melissa downstairs, and she was all excited. I helped Melissa and little Michelle each write a letter to Auntie Joanne. We got them done just in time for my father's arrival. Melissa asked if Auntie Joanne would get these letters. I said most certainly, yes! I told my father what we did, and he just smiled at me and said, "I think Joanne did have a hand in making extra time." The undertaker took the letters and placed them in my sister's casket. Believe me; it helped so much, especially for Melissa. It made Melissa feel that she was able to say good-bye and let her auntie know how she felt about her. It helped both of us with the grief we were feeling. We felt that Joanne really made the time for us to write those letters, to help us with the sadness we all felt.

Chapter Thirty-Two
Psychometry

In psychometry, you can use a person's possession to get a reading about them. If you have a piece of jewelry, you place it in your nondominant hand (the hand you don't write with) and feel the vibrations. Information will come into your head about the person who owned the object. You need to trust the information and symbols that you see or feel. If you do this with a partner, you can take turns to see if your information is accurate. This activity can be done in groups of any size. In a large group, you can each put an item in a basket, and everyone selects one item and relays information to the group and tries to identify who the person is. Don't be discouraged if at first you don't get too much information. Like anything, it gets better with practice.

You can also do photo-psychometry using photographs, holding them and relaying the information that comes to you. This works very nicely, and with practice, the results can be wonderful. This is best done with a deceased loved one's picture. You can get an interesting reading from doing this. Make sure that someone can validate the information, so you can see how accurate it is.

Chapter Thirty-Three
Pairing Off

After opening with a quiet prayer for protection and accuracy, you and a partner sit opposite each other. It may be helpful to lay your hands on top of each other's. Concentrate and start to feel someone coming through. It may feel just like your imagination, but it is usually a person trying to describe himself or herself, giving you a name or telling you who they are. The person can explain how they passed. Sometimes, you may even feel how they died. You might feel a pain in your chest or your head, or even numbness on one side of your body. They will often give you visual symbols like flowers or introduce their pets that have also passed. Their occupations are usually revealed as well. It is very intriguing to figure out who is present. Always ask if there is a message for your partner. If you cannot determine who it is, don't be discouraged because it could be someone your partner just cannot think of at the moment. Later on, you may get validations. The most unlikely people can come through, and you may not realize who they are immediately. Again, practice makes everything better. Keep trying, and it will work because everyone can do this with enough practice.

Chapter Thirty-Four
Shutting Down

When you finish with your mediumship work, you should always shut down. If you don't, spirits can still come into your aura and give you information. When I was first developing as a medium, I didn't know enough to shut down. I was constantly seeing the spirits of people who had passed, and they kept showing me things. I needed to take care of my family and also take care of myself. They need to give you time to live in the physical realm. You need to set limits and close down the spirit world when you are not available. So, when you do open up, you can give it your full attention.

Some mediums tried to show me how to close it down, but for some reason, it did not work. However, one day, I was on the telephone, and they began interrupting by making the phone line filled with static. I was so aggravated that I stomped my left foot down as if I had enough. Suddenly, everything became very quiet and normal. You really have to set limits because you still have your own life to live, and the spirit world needs to know this. They cannot control you, and they will respect your wishes if you tell them. Always work in the white light and protect yourself with the help of your spirit guide.

When you close down mentally, say to the spirit world that you are closing down; you are always protected by the white light. Tell your guide you need his help in closing down, and it will be done.

Chapter Thirty-Five

Faster than Words

I would like to talk about what I have learned from some of the energies I feel. I would be doing a reading, and sometimes, the thoughts come faster than I can speak. I know this could upset a person and have them lose patience with me. I would become very upset because, to me, I seemed as though I was speaking at the right pace. Then, I asked myself, "Why do I talk so fast when I am doing a reading?" I went to one of my friends who has been a medium for a long time and asked if I read too fast. I said, "I really should try to slow down."

She knew I was feeling bad and said, "That' okay. The same thing happens to me. It is the energies that are surrounding you." She told me to remind myself, while doing my reading, to slow down, to take a breath and slow down. This way, people would be able to understand what I was saying in the reading. I have been able to slow down, but it is still very difficult.

One day, I was talking to Will, and he looked at me and said, "Karen, slow down, I cannot understand you."

I took a breath and slowed down. I apologized and said, "Will, the energies sometimes surround me, and the words come out quicker than I want them to." This happens when I am doing a reading. I have to really focus on slowing down and saying the words one at a time.

I remember one time someone asked me to do a reading for a friend. So, just before church, I started with my Rosary. I did this when I had a quiet time, but unfortunately, it was not very long. My husband, Chuck, was ready to give me a ride to church. I jumped out of my chair, grabbed my music, and ran out the door. I did what I needed to do at church, and after a little while, I was able to calm myself down. The person's spirit wanted to speak, and he did.

I learned that some people's energies are stronger than others. This is how the energies come through, and I have learned that this is okay because it takes a lot of energy for them to even say what they have to say. When they show something, even something as simple as a symbol, it takes a lot of energy.

Chapter Thirty-Six
Spirit Guides

One time, someone asked me who our spiritual guides were. I said, they have lived on Earth before and have crossed over to the other side (to the light). We all have them. Some people have one or two, while others have a lot more. They are teachers, doctors, and healers. They can also be Native Americans. My spiritual guides are always telling me to look, listen, speak, and feel—and they have a lot of patience. They also listen a lot. When I do mediumship work, I always ask them to come close, guide me, and keep me safe. They are always there to help me along the way. One of my guides is always telling me to look at the signs and the unexpected phone calls. If you want to hear something funny, they also let me know how my daughter does on her tests. Sometimes, I will write the grade down, and when she comes home from school and shows me her test, I will take the piece of paper out with the test grade that the spirit had shown me, and it is usually right. With a surprised look on her face, my daughter will say, "Mommy, how did you know that?"

My daughter is pretty open to the spiritual gift, so I would say, "They give me the inside scoop." As a result, my daughter never hides her tests from me because she believes the other side will tell me, anyway.

Chapter Thirty-Seven

Symbols of Spirits
(And Other Forms of Spirit Communications)

Bear in mind that symbols mean different things to different people. The same symbol could mean two different things to two different mediums. You need to develop your own "symbol dictionary."

I have been shown symbols that relate to people who have passed over. I have seen a number of items such as a police badge and personal properties or hobbies. Sometimes, I see a person either through a dream or a vision. I can see the outlines of people very clearly and auras that make clear who I am seeing or who they want to communicate with. Sometimes, there is a symbol such as a picture, dogs, or a starfish. To me, this meant that they liked to go to the beach. Black means someone has passed from cancer; blue and red mean someone had passed from heart disease. This is how the other side presented itself to me during a reading for someone, and the information made sense to the person who received the reading. It did not make any sense to me, but for the person who received the reading, the information would make sense to them.

I can also remember one time, during class, at the end of the season, before class broke off for the summer, a spirit moved Tim's cane to the far side of the room. I was happy everyone else heard it. One of the favorite things they do at the Spiritualist Church is show new roses and sunflowers through the vase of old flowers on the platform. I have learned that when I see a flower, a spirit is near. Sometimes, it takes lots of energy for a loved one to manifest itself in the form of symbols to transmit messages.

There are many different ways that we know our family and friends are around. People do not always realize how much energy it takes for a spirit to get a message through. Sometimes, it can be through a scent such as perfume that someone used to wear or their aftershave lotion. You can also know when a spirit is around when there is a sudden temperature change in the room. Sometimes, spirits will take on different forms and show themselves. They have done that to me before. They can also come through dreams. These are called visits. They can come in twinkling lights or orbs or different colors as well—that means the spirit has not fully formed. They can make lightbulbs blink. When I am at my Tuesday night development class, sometimes, the light in the church will blink on and off. It takes a lot of energy. These are just some of the signs you can look for.

Chapter Thirty-Eight

Smells

Smell is another way that our friends and family let us know they are around. It could be through perfume, a cigarette smell, or aftershave lotion. One time, in the fall of 2003, I remember being very busy in the house. Then, all of sudden, I smelled the scent of flowers throughout the house. I had never smelled anything like them before. It was very peaceful and comforting. My husband just looked at me and said, "Karen, its one of those moments." I just smiled at him.

There was another time, during a reading for a client, I asked the person, "Did your grandfather like fishing?"

She said with a smile, "Yes, very much." Then, I told her about the scent of fish that I smelled. I said it was one of the things you could look for.

That is one way people who have crossed over let us know they are around—through a scent or smell. Smells can manifest in various ways. When I was returning home from Medium's Day with Marie one day, we decided to go to a restaurant. Suddenly, I was overwhelmed with the magnificent scent of roses. I asked Marie if she smelled the flowers. She said," Yes, I do, very strongly." To us, it was a symbol that our loved ones on the other side are around us, and we felt that they were happy with the message work we had just completed. They were letting us know that they were around us, too.

Chapter Thirty-Nine

Michelle

One night, I was with my daughter, Melissa, in the kitchen, and my daughter, Michelle, came out to say something. "Mommy," she said, "is that Pa's picture on the refrigerator?"

I answered, "Yes, it is, Michelle."

Then, she said, "Mommy, I see him." Not knowing what she meant, I looked at her. Then, she informed me, "I saw another man with him."

Thinking to myself how children are receptive to spirit, I said, "Oh, I have to go and get Pa's picture." Pa is my grandfather who is in the spirit world.

When I brought the picture out, Michelle looked at it and said, "I saw someone else."

I told Melissa I knew who she was talking about. I went to get the photo album with the wedding pictures. In one particular photo, there is one person who is still alive and three people who have passed away.

The picture is of my grandfather, Uncle Larry, Uncle Joe (who had just passed away), and Uncle Marty (who is still living). During a reading, people often ask if children can see those who have passed away. My answer is yes! As I was getting more pictures, Michelle started telling me about a man who visits her at night when she is asleep. "He looks just like Pa," she told me. However, my father is still on Earth; he has not passed. When I showed Michelle the wedding album, I found the picture of my grandfather. Michelle looked at it and said, "Mommy, that's the man I saw; that's the man who looks just like Pa."

My grandfather died many years before Michelle could recognize him. She thought that was the person who was visiting her at night. While looking at the other pictures, Michelle picked out another uncle who had passed away. Uncle Larry was also someone she had seen. Michelle told me many times that she had seen people, usually family members who have passed on. Michelle always says, "Mommy, I am going to be just like you when I grow up." She also told me that my grandfather makes her smile at night, and that, "Uncle Larry is very nice."

Michelle told me that Uncle Larry wears a brown suit on the other side. I decided to call Aunt Elena because she often wonders if her husband is still around her. She said she hasn't felt him around so much since she moved to her new apartment a few years ago.

When I called my aunt, I told her I had to ask her a question. "Did Uncle Larry have a brown suit that you know of?" I asked.

"Not that I know of," she answered. "He might have had one when he was living with Nana, Jenny, and Pa—when he was younger."

I couldn't help it, so, I said, "Guess what? He does now."

I told her about Michelle and the visits from Uncle Larry. I also decided to tell her who else was visiting Michelle. "You'll never guess who else Michelle sees," I told her.

Michelle often saw Pa at night, in her bedroom. We were both surprised. Even mediums get surprised with the spirit world. My aunt said Michelle didn't even know Pa. Children are very receptive to the spirit world, until someone tells them that they are just imagining things. I reminded her that animals also exhibit the same sense about spirits. As we continued talking, we agreed that it was nice to know that life continues on the other side.

Things had settled down when Michelle came to me and said, "Mommy, there's a baby who is from the other side playing with me. She bothers me. She's not like Uncle Larry or Pa!" Michelle was annoyed by the baby, so I had to teach her what I had learned on my spiritual journey. We got together and held hands. We asked the child who she was with. Was she with an adult who had passed away? A famous British medium had taught me to send spirits to the light if they seemed earth bound.

When we held hands, Michelle asked the baby who she was with. Michelle didn't get an answer. We asked if someone was there to bring the baby to the light. We asked for her guardian angel to come and help her enter the light. As we were praying, Michelle asked, "Baby, can you go to the white light?"

I asked Michelle if the baby went to the white light with an angel, and she said, "Yes." After that, Michelle went back to playing peacefully, without the baby bothering her, so I knew the child had indeed gone to the light. Michelle still comes to me from time to time to tell me about different visitors she had.

If your child comes to you with similar stories, don't just dismiss them. Children really do see the other side. It is us who tell them that it is just a dream or their imagination. From learning and growing as a medium, I now realize that life goes on, and our loved ones do watch over us and try to communicate their presence to us. They are still around, but they are just not physically present anymore.

Chapter Forty
The Little Girl on the Stairs

One night, while I was watching TV, I got very sleepy. I was watching my stairs because sometimes, my stairway gets very busy with people who have passed away. That night, the stairway was particularly busy, and it was lighting up in sparkles of blue and white energy. I never know who is going to appear on the stairs. Sometimes, I feel like my stairway is like a vortex, a place for spirits to enter and to leave. This night was different from most nights. It felt like someone was staring at me, but I did not know who it was. That's why I had to learn to trust what is called clairsentience or the ability to feel the presence of spirits. But I was just too tired to even go to sleep, so I said my prayers and asked the Blessed Mother to keep me safe. After that, I turned the light off and went into a deep sleep. Around 2:30 in the morning, I woke up because I felt like something was staring at me, and sure enough, there she was, looking down at me, a little girl. The little girl startled me and took me off guard. She was as cute as a button. She had curly, brown hair down to her shoulders that glowed and the prettiest brown eyes. She wore a T-shirt and underwear, and she was around four years old. She smiled at me. After a couple of minutes, she just disappeared. I had to remember what she looked like, and I got a piece of paper to write everything down. I know it takes a lot of energy for spirits to come through to show themselves.

After that, I went upstairs to bed and went to sleep. When my friend came to pick me up for my Tuesday night class, nobody could understand about the girl I had seen. So, I let it go for a while. We broke off for a week because my teacher was going to Florida for a week's vacation.

I decided to call my hairdresser, Lisa, to make an appointment to get my hair colored. Saturday came, and I had to get everyone up because I had an early appointment with Lisa. Lisa and I got talking, and she is very open to spirits. She asked me if I could read her, so I said okay. All at once, someone from the other side was nagging at me, and the hairdresser was lighting up in sparkles of white energy.

Then, I started telling Lisa about the little girl on the stairs and describing her to Lisa. She did not understand the information that I was giving her, but she called her mother who said the little girl's name was Marie. Her mother could understand all the information about the little girl. "She had passed away a long time ago," Lisa's mother said. Lisa told me, the next time I saw her, how her mother could understand all the information about the little girl and validated everything about the little girl. I felt so much better, knowing that the little girl belonged to someone.

Then, I told Lisa she was fine in the spirit world and in the white light on the other side. We both smiled at each other, and then, I came home.

I never know whom I am going to wake up to or find during the night, whether it be on my stairway or in my bedroom. I am just happy whenever I could find out who the children belonged to when they do come for a visit from the other side. Also, I learned in class from an English medium, whose name is John Carol, that I should ask the children who they are with, and to make sure that they are not alone. I thanked Lisa for validating the information about the little girl on the stairs and the little girl for letting her family know that she was okay on the other side, and that she was happy.

Chapter Forty-One
Seeing Lena

One night, two of my friends and I were visiting another friend at her home. Everything was beautiful and quiet. I always feel welcome at her house. There were candles burning on a beautiful, summer night.

We were all enjoying each other's conversation and talking about many things. The evening continued on, when all of a sudden, an elderly woman's face appeared. She had short and thick black hair, and it had a little wave to it. Her eyes were dark, and she had a round, healthy-looking face. It appeared as though she was enjoying our conversation. As quickly as she had appeared, she disappeared.

It was late, so we ended the night and all went home. I went to bed with warm thoughts of the evening. The next day, when I woke up, I decided to call Fran. I know it takes a lot of energy for spirits to show themselves, and this woman's energy was very nice. I felt it was important to tell Fran about this and what I had seen. I explained to Fran what I had seen, and Fran told me that it was her mother who had crossed over. Fran said that her son had seen her mother, and she had shown herself the exact same way. We said good-bye, until we could get together again.

Chapter Forty-Two

The Gift

One time, at choir practice, I can remember Pat and I were talking. Pat told me about her friend, Jill, who was a Reiki master. A Reiki healer is one who is trained to perform hands-on healing to individuals who need it. Pat invited me and another friend out to lunch the next day. I agreed to go, but I had to bring my daughter, Michelle, who was in preschool. After a snowstorm the previous night, the next day looked like winter wonderland. But, Pat and Ann came anyway. We decided to go to the Hingham Bay Club for lunch. We were all talking and having fun. Even Michele was extra good that day.

When we got to the restaurant, we went inside. It was not too fancy, but it was very pleasant. After we sat down, Jill arrived, and we were all introduced. During our conversation, Pat told Jill that I was a clairvoyant medium, and that I could see things both inside and outside my mind's eye. She told Jill that I could see people who had passed. I tried to act as normal as possible because not everyone believes in mediumship.

As we continued to talk, Pat told a waitress in the restaurant about me. People from the other side came through to give me information for her. It all started to make sense to her. Then, more information came through for another person who worked there at the restaurant. Then, Claudia was in a message I was given, so Pat went to get Claudia. When Claudia came over and was given a message from her deceased family, she didn't validate it. She just didn't answer or give me any indication that she knew who I was talking about. After the waitresses left, Pat asked me why Claudia would not affirm that it was her family. I said, "Not everyone believes in mediumship or even that people are still around after they pass on to the other side." I do not get discouraged because I feel that if they make the effort to send a message to their loved one, the least I can do is deliver it, whether they accept it or not.

I can remember going to a workshop one time, with one of the English mediums who told us that even when the client says "no" to a reading, they really do understand what you are telling them. Sometimes, when they go home and reflect on it, they would realize that they really did hear from the other side. You do want your client to be happy with the reading, even if it is unexpected, like Claudia. But you must learn to trust the spirits and just let the information go.

After lunch, Jill asked if I would like to go to Plymouth with her on Friday night. So, I went to Plymouth on that cold and crisp evening. We went to her friend's house, where we had a class. We were all introduced when we got there. The teacher paired us off, but we did not know who we would be reading because she was going to blindfold us. I wasn't sure if I liked that idea, but I thought I better try it after coming so far. Everyone had a turn doing a reading while I watched. Finally, there was a very good psychic who was going to give me a reading. When she first started to read, it did not make sense, and then, suddenly, everything clicked. She said that when I was young, I was shy and felt alone. She also said that I could see people around me, could feel them, and sense them, but no one else did. As the reading continued, I stood dumbfounded and surprised at all the information she was giving me. She also asked if I always felt uncomfortable around others. By this time, I was at a loss for words. She told me I was very gifted, and that I would use my gift in the future.

Then, she removed the blindfold, so she could see who she was reading. We began to discuss the reading, and she told me that I always had the gift, but didn't understand it until the past few years. I told her she was right. She also told me there was something special with the gift and how I was supposed to use it. All I could say is that she was correct again. I told her how I always tried to fluff off the mediumship because it wasn't a normal thing. That night, I got a big affirmation of my spiritual gifts; however, I decided not to go back to that group. I decided to stay with my class at the Spiritual Church.

I now realize that we all have gifts—but in many different forms. Not everyone will understand these gifts, but that is all right with me. Jill called to say she received my message about not going back to her group. She said that she understood I had my own special "group of psychics" that I felt comfortable with. I thanked her for the experience, and that was the last time I heard from Jill.

Chapter Forty-Three
What It Is Like on the Other Side

When we pass over to the other side, I know our families and friends who have gone before us are there waiting to help us make the transition from this life to the next.

We begin our spiritual journey with the help of our family members and friends who have gone to the other side before us. They welcome us and help us adjust to our new environment. It is beautiful, calm, and peaceful over there. Sometimes, I don't want them to tell me about the brilliant colors and beauty there. When it is my turn, I would like to experience this phenomenon for myself. I need to wait and see what God has in mind for me. Some people believe God is a man; some believe God is genderless. I believe that God is a loving, caring Being. That is what I have been told by spirits from the other side.

Our families are usually there to help us if we ask. The problem is that we cannot always hear them. That's when it is a good idea to seek out a medium. Sometimes, loved ones may be involved in other matters on the other side and are not available presently. If that is the case, they will usually send another spirit to give a message or to let you know they are around. People who have passed over are always anxious to communicate with us. There are many things occurring on the other side. They live in a different time frame than we do. In fact, time does not exist on the other side. Time is a multidimensional space.

For a long time, I did not hear from my sister after she passed. Finally, I realized that she was involved in her own readjustment. As soon as she was able, she let me know that she was around. It took about six months for her to contact me. I have to remind myself that they are busy, too.

Many people don't realize that it takes a lot of energy for people to come through. When they do come, they show themselves to me and usually describe how they died. Often, I can feel what happened to them in my body. It can be very uncomfortable. If it was a heart attack, I will feel chest pains. If it was a stroke, I often feel a bad headache and even paralysis on the appropriate side. If a person had passed violently, I will know that, too. They tell me these things so that the person I am giving the message to can validate that it is really their loved one. Sometimes, it can be the smallest detail that will have the greatest impact on the client.

This process helps the loved ones feel relieved and peaceful that their loved ones are still "around." If a child has passed, a parent can be grateful that they are all right and happy on the other side. Indeed, life goes on! Most people do want to know that someone dear to them is still available to them. Oftentimes, amends could be made from the other side. Good-byes that were never said could be voiced. But there is no reason to say good-bye because you can still communicate, though in a different manner. Also, on the other side, when we die of a sudden death, such as a heart attack, on an airplane, or a car accident, we do not realize that our spirits leave our human bodies. Our families, who have passed away, are there to take us to a healing center to help make the transition from the physical to the spiritual world.

Chapter Forty-Four

The Fashion Show

One day, my mother called to ask me if I would like to go to a fashion show that the Lion's Club was having. I really didn't feel like going, but I decided to go. My mother asked if Melissa would like to come. Melissa agreed to go with us, even though we thought it would be boring. We decided to go for Grandma's sake.

The fashion show took place at Lombardo's Restaurant in Randolph, Massachusetts. When we got there, we met my mother upstairs. It was at that time when I suddenly remembered something. "Oh my goodness," I exclaimed, turning to my daughter, "I forgot to shut down the spirit." To shut down from the spirit, I have to stomp my left foot or the other side will ask me to give messages to those around me. The best way for me to shut down is to stomp my left foot. I could also feel vibrations from those people around me. We approached my mother; she was with two of her friends.

My mother told them that I had been a Carmelite nun and how I would have been a very good one if I had stayed in the convent. My mother didn't realize we were there, so I told her, "I heard what you said." She smiled at me, and I looked at my daughter and told her, "God had other plans in store for me." Little did she know about my mediumistic abilities and how strong and vibrant they were. My mother didn't know that I belonged to the Spiritualist Church, and that I was a platform medium.

As we were walking, I told Melissa that the convent was a learning experience for me. I was only there for over a year, but I learned a lot about myself and my spiritual life. As we walked into the room where the fashion show was being held, I told Melissa that I had to act as normal as possible because my mother does not understand my abilities, neither does she condone them. Then, I asked Melissa, "What is normal anyway?"

As the show went on, one of my mother's friends came over, and we were introduced. We talked about multiple sclerosis since her daughter and I both have this ailment. We discussed the medications we were taking, and she told me how great I looked for someone who was diagnosed with the disease. I told her that I have been in remission for six years. My neurologist told me to, "Do what you have to do in life while you can." I took his advice and pursued my gift as a medium. My mother was not open to this idea. I had to keep it a secret in order to have a relationship with her. Every day, when I wake up, I thank God for a brand-new day. I am happy that I am able to walk, to see, and to do all the things I love.

The fashion show continued. One of my mother's friends had a picture of someone dear to her who had passed away. She told us that her granddaughter carries her grandfather's picture with her everywhere she goes, even to church. As the conversation continued, something kept nagging at me, but I knew I couldn't say anything because my mother is not enlightened to mediumship. My mother's friend continued talking about her late husband, and she wondered if he was listening to her granddaughter's prayers. She really seemed to need some answers.

I asked Melissa what my mother was doing. When I found out she was talking to someone else, I had the opportunity to give my mother's friend a message. I told her that her husband was with her granddaughter all the time, and he was watching over her.

She looked at me and smiled. She looked more at peace knowing that information. She was very happy to hear that her husband was watching over his family. "Isn't it wonderful to know that our loved ones watch us from the other side?" I told her.

Chapter Forty-Five
The Story Within the Story

When I first started writing this book, it was not an easy task for me because I had such horrible handwriting. Nobody could understand it. When I started, Chuck's sister-in-law, Ruthie, helped me with the best that she could. Then, I put it away. This book started out as a journal. But something kept on nagging at me to write down what was going on, in case someone was going through the same thing. Then, they would know that they were not going crazy. After Ruthie couldn't help me anymore, I put my journal away. However, when I was singing in the church choir at the Our Lady of Good Counsel in Quincy, Massachusetts, some of the church members knew that I was a medium. There were also a couple of church members who didn't know that I was a medium. One person whom I got to know during that year, whose name is Pat, agreed to help me.

I knew I had horrible handwriting, but it wasn't always that way. Pat told me she was going on a trip to Las Vegas, and she was going to take my stories with her. When she came home, she came over and said, "Karen, I have something to tell you. We were in a car accident, and my briefcase is in the car with all your stories in it." I told her that was okay, but the papers for the book were gone for a long time. One night, at choir practice, Pat came in and said, "Karen, I have your papers and journal for your book. They came home today." I told her that I would be happy to take them off her hands because I knew Pat was a very busy person, and I knew it would be too much for her. So then, I brought the journal and the stories home and kept them in a safe place.

At Easter time in 2003, I was talking to my closest girlfriend, Nadia, and I told her about the book that I started writing. She was very interested and open, which made it extra nice. She said, "Karen, I would like to do the typing for you." I thanked her, but I told her one thing: I have horrible handwriting. She told me that it was okay, and that maybe the book would help her. It was nice because Nadia's grandmother started coming through with a message for her. I told her to tell me if she could or could not understand the information that I was receiving. She could understand everything. This took place a couple of years ago.

During a reading, the information coming in from spirits comes so fast that someone has to have a piece of paper and a pen to write the information down because I will not remember the information afterward. Time went on, and I didn't hear from Nadia for the longest time. When I called her, she didn't return any of my phone calls. I told Chuck I had a bad feeling about this.

Finally, one day, my cousin, Steven, called me and said, "Karen, I have something to tell you." Then, Nadia got on the phone and told me, "I have something really bad to tell you." Nadia is so nice that you just cannot say anything mean to her.

She told me she had lost all of the paperwork that I had given her. She lost the whole stack of papers that were on her desk. I told her it was okay, and that maybe the papers had only been misplaced.

After I was done on the phone, Chuck just looked at me, and I told him, "You do not want to know all that I have just heard." So, I went out on the back porch, got my radio, put my CD on, and started all over again. And I do mean *all over again*. I found that I could recall most of the stories in the book, but the most important stories that I had obtained permission from were stories from people who had passed away.

Then, I took the papers I had already rewritten, threw them up in the air, and said, "I give up." I closed the back porch door and left the pages there. I even threw some of them out.

My daughter, Melissa, who, when I think about it, I realize is very wise beyond her years, just looked at me and told me, "Mommy, you can't give up. You are always telling us there are no quitters in the family, no matter how hard it gets. God only gives us what we can handle."

I gazed at the serious look on her face and told her, "You are right; there are no quitters in this family."

Then, she told me, "Mommy, you have something special to share with people who may be just like you." So, I went to the trash bin, got the pages back, and, having not been out on the porch for three days, was surprised to find all the pages were still there.

Chuck didn't throw the pages out, not one. My husband doesn't understand any of this, but he knows there is something to all of it.

So, as I was saying, when I saw the papers there untouched, I thought that, maybe, it was meant to be.

Then, I decided to call my friend, Sandy, who is very psychic. I asked, "Can you sense anything about my book? Did Nadia lose it?" Sandy got very quiet on the phone.

Then, Sandy asked me if she could call me back. I told her it was fine. Well, about an hour went by, and the phone rang. She told me to call Nadia right away and to tell her the book was in a stack of paper. I got off the phone with Sandy and quickly called Nadia. She was home, and I gave her Sandy's message. When I got off the phone with her, I told my friend, Fran, what happened. She told me to ask her mother, Lena, for help. She lived in Lawrence at one time. Usually, I don't like to bother the spirits about anything, but Fran was always telling me that it is okay to ask the spirits for help. So, I did ask Fran's mother for help.

The next day, while at work, Chuck got a phone call from Nadia. She had found all my papers, and I do mean all of them.

They were in the place Sandy had told me they would be—they were in a stack of papers. Steven, Nadia's boyfriend, told Chuck that he would bring them in that week, before they get misplaced again. Then, I looked up and thanked Lena for all her help. I got on the phone with Sandy and told her that Nadia had found the papers where she had told me they would be.

I thought it was important for Sandy to know that she was correct in the validation of her gifts. Then, when Chuck brought home all the papers, it was like Christmas day all over again. When I saw all the stories, I was so happy and overjoyed that I looked up toward the heavens and kissed all the stories. It was like getting an old friend back.

When I was talking to Sandy the next day on the phone, I told her that I did not even know why I was writing. Then, she said, "Karen, don't you realize by now that you have a story to tell?"

So, I just listened to what she was saying. Then, I asked her, "Do you want to know something?" I said. "Even this part could be a part of the book because of the things you have helped me realize about writing my story."

Then, Sandy said to me, "You are always telling me that you are like wine waiting to be fermented."

Isn't that the truth?

So, after that time, I always made sure that my journal and my papers are in a safe place because it is like having an old friend around. Sometimes, I get busy doing everyday things, but I have learned to continue with my book. I can remember one night falling asleep on the couch and being awakened by something that was touching me. I looked up, and there was a piece of paper that showed itself. I couldn't understand any of the handwriting that was on it. Then, I began chuckling to myself because it was about 4:30 in the morning when I saw the paper. Do you want to know something? My handwriting wasn't clear at all. Then, I thanked whoever it was in the spirit world that was showing me the paper.

Just knowing that the other side is listening to us, even if something is missing, if you are writing a book, or you have lost something, you can ask for some spiritual help as long as it is within reason.

Chapter Forty-Six
Baby Flo

One night, while I was sleeping soundly, I was suddenly awakened by a soft touch on my shoulder. When I looked at the corner of the bedroom, I saw a small spirit manifest itself. It happened to be a small child, about one year old. There was something different about this child from others I have seen. She was dressed in a pure white bonnet and nightdress. But the most surprising thing that was she was sleeping peacefully on a cloud. This precious baby communicated with me with her mind. She told me that she lived in the eighteenth century, and just as suddenly, disappeared. I had a feeling that she was visiting from the cemetery across the street.

The next day, I told my fourteen-year-old daughter, Melissa, about what happened. Melissa knew from historical readings that that was how children were buried at that time. Something strongly urged Melissa to go to the cemetery and look at the gravestones.

While Melissa was looking for a baby's tombstone from the seventeen hundreds, I called a friend who is also a medium. Mike Woods has collaborated on many occasions to help find spirits. Mike felt that it was strange for a baby to be buried alone at that time. I told Mike I would let him know later what we discovered.

Within minutes, Melissa returned home with a surprised look on her face. She told me that she found the baby's headstone, from an eighteenth-century grave. Another interesting thing caught Melissa's attention. The baby was the only one from that timeframe. All of the other gravestones were from the twentieth century. This was quite unusual, to say the least. The baby's name was Florence, and she lived for only a year.

I called Mike and told him what we had discovered. I also told him how peaceful and very happy "Flo" was. She had just popped in to visit and say hello. She was also reminding us that life goes on, even for babies on the other side.

About a month later, my father-in-law passed away. Melissa wanted to go for a walk in the neighborhood cemetery. I told her I would go with her. She wanted to show me where "Baby Flo's" grave was. When we found the grave, I realized that, again, it was my birthday, and I was in a cemetery. I believe it was "Baby Flo" saying happy birthday to me and thanking me for taking such an interest in her. I knew then that on special occasions, I always ended up in one cemetery or another. It seems to be my calling—to visit with the spirit world and carry messages to the living, even on my birthday.

Even now, I perceive the spirit world around me and others daily. I see, feel, hear, and smell the spirit world naturally. I hope to bring comfort to people by receiving messages from loved ones on the other side.

One thing I have noticed is that the veil between the worlds is thinning. More and more people are becoming aware of the spirit world. Individuals are becoming very interested in life after death. In the past, it was considered inappropriate to seek news from the other side. Now, it is evident that more people are open to the spirits and are visiting mediums and clairvoyants at an ever-increasing rate.

It is comforting to know that we continue on even if we are no longer physical. A medium can help with confirming this knowledge by giving evidence or proof that the spirit world thrives.

Our loved ones are not forgotten.

Chapter Forty-Seven
Glossary for Spirit Communication

Aura: It is a permanent radiation around the body and produced by the nervous system. Allegedly, bands of colored light surround the body of humans, plants, and animals. It is referred to by clairvoyants as the etheric body.

Automatic Writing: It is writing without the agent's volition and, sometimes, without their knowledge. (Encyclopedia of Occultism)

Clairaudience: This is clear hearing. The power or faculty of hearing something not present to the ear but regarded as having objective reality; extrasensory information that is perceived by sound. (Contemporary Definitions of Psychic Phenomena and Related Subjects)

Clairsentience: This is clearly sensing a projection onto the sense of perception; sometimes considered as man's "sixth sense." It includes a wide range of extrasensory awareness and detecting the presence of spirit.

Clairvoyance: This is a psychic's ability to see or sense what is not in sight, including objects or events. These may include spirit presences and appearances of objects or events without sensory means, clear seeing, or psychic sight.

Independent Music: This is when an instrument plays without the aid of a physical musician. D. D. Howe was reported to place his hands on an accordion with the keys facing down, and the instrument would begin to play and, eventually, move around the room by itself.

Materialization: This is to appear suddenly; to make a spirit or object appear in physical form.

Physical Mediumship: This is objective in nature and works directly with the five senses.

Rapping, writing by planchette, independent music, trumpet communication, independent typewriting, spirit materialization, rapports, passing matter through matter, magnetic healing, transfiguration, independent voice, levitation.

Precognitive Dreams: This is either realistic or symbolic information concerning the future received through dreams.

Mental Mediumship: This appeal directly to the intellect, inspirational writing or speaking, spiritual healing, clairvoyance, clairaudience, trans-speaking, speaking in tongues, prophecy, clairsentience, and psychometry.

Overshadow: This is similar to transfiguration. The spirit entity appears to be over the medium and sometimes visible to others.

Karen Miranda is a clairvoyant and clairsentient medium who delivers messages from the spirit world. She is the mother of three and lives in Quincy, Massachusetts. Karen has been capable of seeing spirits since she was a child. She has studied and developed her gift of mediumship for the past six years at the Spiritualist Church and continues to give private, as well as group readings to many. Karen is also known as a platform medium: someone who can give messages to a small group of people at the same time. Karen continues to practice spirit mediumship in various places throughout the state.